ent Garden Gallery,
Russell Street,
don WC3 5HP
1977

SCHOTT

Designer: Keith Cheetham
Production Director: Rick Wentworth

Printed in Great Britain by
Caligraving Limited,
Thetford, Norfolk

Boston 3rd April 1977

My dear Michael,

This exhibition is a way
of saying "Thank you": for your music and
for your music-making; for the example
you have set us of a creative mind true
to itself in the face of the changing
fashions of our uncertain times; for the
problems you have set us in the
performance of your works and the freedom
you have allowed us in our efforts to
realize what your imagination has
prompted you to set down on paper; for
your insistence that, to misquote your
favourite Blake, we hear through the ear,
not with it; but most of all your faith
that the workings of the intellect are as
nothing without reference to the heart.

You are fond of quotations:
may I end with one? Long may you
". through the terrible novelty of light,
stalk on, stalk on!

Colin Davis

Exhibition Committee

Colin Davis
Chairman

Michael Vyner
Vice Chairman

John Amis
Meirion Bowen
Russell Brown
David Cairns
Keith Cheetham
Geoffrey Crankshaw
William Drummond
Barrie Gavin
Sally Groves
Betty Scholar
Rick Wentworth
Eric Walter White
Katharine Wilkinson
John Woolf

Contents

Chronology

1905   MICHAEL KEMP TIPPETT born on 2 January in a London nursing home, second son of Henry William Tippett (a retired lawyer and proprietor of a hotel at Cannes in the south of France) and Isabel Clementina Binny Kemp. Tippett's father was Cornish in origin, his mother Kentish. Later in 1905 the family moved from Eastcote, Middlesex to the small village of Wetherden in Suffolk, where they remained until 1919. Because of financial difficulties Tippett's parents lived abroad from 1919 to 1932.

1914-1922   Schooling: Brookfield Preparatory School, Swanage, Dorset; Fettes College, Edinburgh; Stamford Grammar School, Lincolnshire.

1923-1928   Royal College of Music, London: composition (Charles Wood and C. H. Kitson), piano (Aubin Raymar), conducting (Malcolm Sargent and Adrian Boult). Gains degree of B.Mus.

1924-1931   Conductor of a madrigal group, and a concert and operatic society promoted by Oxted and Limpsfield Players, an amateur dramatic society performing at the Barn Theatre, Oxted, Surrey.

Operatic productions included Vaughan Williams's *The Shepherds of the Delectable Mountains*, Tippett's own realization of the 18th century ballad opera *The Village Opera* and Stanford's *The Travelling Companion.*

Concerts included Handel's *Messiah* (15th November 1931) and one devoted to his own music (5 April 1930). After the latter he decided his compositional technique was inadequate and that he would take lessons again.

1929-1951   Lives in Oxted.

1929-1932   Part-time schoolmaster (teaching French, with a little class music) at Hazelwood School, Limpsfield.

1930-1932   Further period of study at Royal College of Music, with R. O. Morris.

1932-1933   Invited to take charge of music at work-camps near Boosbeck, a small mining village in the Cleveland district of North Yorkshire. The Camps, initiated by Rolf Gardiner, were designed to help unemployed ironstone miners gain some independence and solvency by encouraging the growth of a land economy and of a local culture. At Boosbeck Tippett directed performances, with local people taking part, of *The Beggar's Opera* (1932) and his own folk-song opera *Robin Hood* (1933).

After firsthand experience of the depression and the effects of unemployment, Tippett gave up schoolteaching and undertook two jobs, both more closely linked with his developing interest in left-wing politics.

1932-1940   Conductor of South London (Morley College) Orchestra, formed to enable professional musicians, put out of work by the depression and the advent of the "talkies", to keep in practice. The orchestra, about 45 strong, rehearsed in Morley College which was the centre for activities helping the unemployed in South London, and gave concerts generally of popular classics in the College and in halls, theatres, schools, parks and churches in South London. Concert income was divided among the players. Tippett himself was employed by the then London County Council.

1932-1939	Directed two choirs sponsored by the Royal Arsenal Co-operative Society, one at Abbey Wood near Woolwich, the other at New Malden. The RACS was affiliated to the Labour Party and Tippett became involved in this work through his friendship with Alan Bush and Francesca Allinson, both conductors of choirs associated with the working-class movement. Tippett's choirs were initially encouraged to sing "political songs" of the type pioneered by Eisler in pre-Hitler Germany, though later he yielded to popular pressure and gave performances of light opera.
1934-1938	Trotsky sympathiser, though not a member of any Trotskyite party. Joined the Communist Party for a few months in 1935 but left, when he realised he would not succeed in converting his party branch to Trotskyism. Active interest in Trotskyism began to wane when he saw that left-wing politics was unable to offer any answer to the barbarities of Nazism or Communism.
1937-1939	Friendship with T. S. Eliot, who encouraged Tippett to write his own text for the oratorio *A Child or Our Time.*
1938-1939	Renewed interest in the writings of C. G. Jung. After a short period with the Jungian analyst John Layard, Tippett conducted his own self-analysis.
1939-1940	With the outbreak of war and suspension of adult education, he lost income from the RACS choirs and returned to schoolmastering (teaching classics at Hazelwood).
1940-1945	Joined the Peace Pledge Union in 1940, the pacifist union founded in 1935 by Rev. Dick Sheppard. Also in 1940 he applied for provisional registration as a conscientious objector. His case was not heard by the local tribunal until 1942, when he was given non-combatant military duties. On appeal he was given conditional registration. He refused to comply with the conditions and was eventually sentenced, on 21 June 1943, to three months imprisonment.
	In 1940 he was invited by Eva Hubback, principal of Morley College, to become Director of Music at the College, shortly after the building had been almost completely destroyed by a high explosive bomb (15 October 1940). Under Tippett musical life picked up again and in a short time Morley's teaching staff included such figures as Walter Goehr, Matyas Seiber and Walter Bergmann; Tippett himself directed the choir. Monthly chamber concerts, featuring music by Purcell, Gibbons, Dowland, Monteverdi, Stravinsky, Hindemith, Britten and Tippett, became important events in the London musical calender. Performers included the Amadeus Quartet, Benjamin Britten, Alfred Deller, Noel Newton-Wood and Peter Pears.
1945-1951	Tippett played a major role in Peace Pledge Union affairs, speaking at several meetings. In 1946 the Morley College Concerts Society was formed, in order to promote performances of large-scale works. Monteverdi's *Vespers*, for instance, was given its first British performance in 1946. Having discovered that he could earn a reasonable secondary income as a broadcaster for the BBC, Tippett resigned from Morley College in 1951, in order to devote more time to composition.
1951-1960	Lived in Tidebrook Manor, Wadhurst, Sussex. Continued broadcasting, lecturing and conducting. In 1958 he edited a number of broadcast talks, together with other writings, to form a

book, *Moving into Aquarius*. He was elected chairman of the Peace Pledge Union in 1957, President in 1958 — a position he still holds.

1960-1970   Lived at Parkside, Corsham, Wilts.

1965   Patron and conductor of the Leicestershire Schools Symphony Orchestra. First visit to the U.S.A. in July, 1965, when he was 'Composer in Residence' at the Aspen Festival.

1969-1974   Artistic Director of Bath Festival.

1970   Moved to new house on the Marlborough Downs.

Ian Kemp 1977

5

8

12

13

Chronological List of Compositions

Some Early Unpublished Works

c. 1928	*String Quartet in F minor*
1928-1930	*Concerto in D* for Flutes, Oboe, Horns & Strings
1928	*String Quartet in F major* revised 1930
	Songs for Voice and Piano on texts by Charlotte Mary Mew *Sea Love* *Afternoon Tea* *Arracombe Wood*
1929	*The Village Opera* Ballad Opera in 3 acts with text and music composed and arranged by the composer
1930	*Psalm in C* — The Gateway for chorus and small orchestra text by Christopher Fry
1930	Incidental Music to Flecker's *'Don Juan'*
1932	*String Trio in B flat*
1933/4	*Symphony in B flat*
1934	*Symphony in B flat* revised version
1934	*Robin Hood* Ballad Opera, dialogue by David Ayerst, lyrics by Ruth Pennyman
1937	*A Song of Liberty* for chorus and orchestra text from *'The Marriage of Heaven and Hell'* by William Blake.
c. 1937	*Miners* for chorus and piano text by Judy Wogan. Written for a Trade Union pageant of English history at the Crystal Palace organised by Alan Bush.
1938	*Robert of Sicily* Opera for Children, text by Christopher Fry adapted from Robert Downing, music arranged by the composer.
1939	*Seven at one stroke* A Play for Children, text by Christopher Fry, music arranged by the composer.

Published Works

1934-35	*String Quartet No. 1* revised 1943 'To Wilfred Franks' First performed by the Brosa Quartet at a Lemare Concert, Mercury Theatre, London, December 1935: revised version by The Zorian Quartet, Wigmore Hall, London, February 1944 (In the revised version, a new first movement replaces the original first and second movements)
1936-37	*Sonata for Piano* revised 1942 and 1954 'To Francesca Allinson' First performed by Phyllis Sellick, Queen Mary Hall, London, November 1937 (In the revised version, the original 5th variation of the first movement is shortened)
1938-39	*Concerto for Double String Orchestra* 'To Jeffrey Mark' First performed by the South London Orchestra conducted by the composer, Morley College, London, April 1940

1939-41	*Fantasia on a Theme of Handel for Piano and Orchestra* 'To Phyllis Sellick' First performed by Phyllis Sellick and the Walter Goehr Orchestra conducted by Walter Goehr, Wigmore Hall, March 1942 (The theme is taken from the Prelude to the Air with Variations in Handel's 'Suites de pièces pour le clavecin', Vol. 2 (*c.* 1733), as quoted by Samuel Butler in *Erewhon*)
1939-41	*A Child of Our Time* Oratorio for SATB soloists, chorus and orchestra, with text by the composer First performed by Joan Cross, Margaret McArthur, Peter Pears, Roderick Lloyd, London Region Civil Defence Choir and Morley College Choir and the London Philharmonic Orchestra conducted by Walter Goehr, Adelphi Theatre, London, March 1944
1941-42	*String Quartet No. 2 in F sharp* 'To Walter Bergmann' First performed by the Zorian Quartet, Wigmore Hall, March 1943
1942	*Two Madrigals* for unaccompanied chorus SATB: The Windhover (poem by Gerard Manley Hopkins) The Source (poem by Edward Thomas) 'To Morley College Choir' First performed by the Morley College Choir conducted by Walter Bergmann, Morley College, July 1943
1943	*Boyhood's End* Cantata on a text by W. H. Hudson for tenor and piano 'To Peter Pears and Benjamin Britten' First performed by Peter Pears and Benjamin Britten, Morley College, June 1943
1943	*Fanfare No. 1* for 4 horns, 3 trumpets and 3 trombones *Written for the 50th anniversary of the consecration of St Matthew's Church, Northampton* First performed, September 1943
1943	*Plebs Angelica* Motet for double chorus 'For the choir of Canterbury Cathedral, January 1944' *Commissioned by Canterbury Cathedral* First performed by the Fleet Street Choir conducted by T. B. Lawrence, Canterbury Cathedral, September 1944
1944	*The Weeping Babe* Motet for soprano solo and unaccompanied chorus SATB (poem by Edith Sitwell) 'In memory of Bronwen Wilson, August 8th 1944' *Commissioned by the B.B.C. for 'Poet's Christmas' 1944* First performed by Margaret Ritchie and Morley College Choir conducted by the composer, The Polytechnic, Regent Street, London, December 1944
1944-45	*Symphony No. 1* First performed by the Liverpool Philharmonic Orchestra conducted by Malcolm Sargent, Philharmonic Hall, Liverpool, November 1945
1945-46	*String Quartet No. 3* 'To Mrs Mary Behrend' *Commissioned by Mary Behrend* First performed by the Zorian Quartet, Wigmore Hall, October 1946
1946	*Preludio Al Vespro di Monteverdi* for organ 'For Geraint Jones' Written to precede a performance of Monteverdi's *Vespers* 1610, Central Hall, Westminster, November 1946; first performed by Geraint Jones (A fragment of the plainsong melody *Sancta Maria* and the whole melody of *Ave Maris Stella* are used as material for the Prelude)

1946	*Little Music* for string orchestra
	'For the 10th anniversary of the Jacques String Orchestra'
	First performed by the Jacques Orchestra conducted by Reginald Jacques, Wigmore Hall, November 1946

1946-52	*The Midsummer Marriage* Opera in 3 acts with text by the composer
	First performed by the Covent Garden Opera, conducted by John Pritchard, produced by Christopher West, with scenery and costumes by Barbara Hepworth and choreography by John Cranko, Royal Opera House, Covent Garden, January 1955

Ritual Dances from *The Midsummer Marriage* for orchestra with optional chorus
'To Walter Goehr'
First performed by the Basel Kammerorchester conducted by Paul Sacher, Basel, February 1953

1948	*Suite for the Birthday of Prince Charles* (Suite in D)
	Commissioned by the B.B.C. in celebration of the birth of Prince Charles
	First performed by the B.B.C. Symphony Orchestra conducted by Sir Adrian Boult, November 1948
	(The first movement is a chorale prelude on the hymn tune 'Crimond'; the second uses a traditional French melody; the third the march from Act 1 of *The Midsummer Marriage* and an Irish version of 'All round my hat'; the fourth the English medieval hymn 'Angelus ad Virginem'; and the last 'Early one morning', the Helston Furry Dance, a 'folk' tune of the composer's and material re-worked from the overture to *Robin Hood*)

1950-51	*The Heart's Assurance* Song-Cycle for high voice and piano (poems by Sydney Keyes and Alun Lewis)
	'In memory of Francesca Allinson (1902-1945)'
	Commissioned by Peter Pears
	First performed by Peter Pears and Benjamin Britten, Wigmore Hall, May 1951

1952	*Dance, Clarion Air* Madrigal for five voices SSATB with text by Christopher Fry
	From the collection of songs for mixed voices, A Garland for the Queen, *commissioned by the Arts Council of Great Britain to mark the occasion of the Coronation of Her Majesty Queen Elizabeth II, of which the composers were Bax, Berkeley, Bliss, Finzi, Howells, Ireland, Rawsthorne, Rubbra, Tippett & Vaughan Williams*
	First performed by the Golden Age Singers and the Cambridge University Madrigal Society conducted by Boris Ord, Royal Festival Hall, London, June 1953

1953	*Fantasia Concertante on a Theme of Corelli* for string orchestra
	Commissioned by the Edinburgh Festival 1953, *in celebration of the tercentenary of the birth of Arcangelo Corelli*
	First performed by the B.B.C. Symphony Orchestra conducted by the composer, Usher Hall, Edinburgh, August 1953
	(The theme is taken from the *Adagio/Vivace* section from the first movement of Corelli's Concerto Grosso in F, Op. 6, No. 2)

1953	*Fanfare No. 2* for 4 trumpets
1953	*Fanfare No. 3* for 3 trumpets
	Written for the St. Ives Festival of Arts, June 1953

1953-54	*Divertimento on 'Sellinger's Round'* for Chamber Orchestra
	'Dedicated to Paul Sacher'
	Commissioned by Paul Sacher
	First performed by the Collegium Musicum Zürich conducted by Paul Sacher, Zürich, November 1954
	(A variation of the traditional tune 'Sellinger's Round' appears in all five movements. Incorporated in the movements are quotations from a Gibbons Fantasia, Dido's first song in Purcell's *Dido and Aeneas*, the song 'Preach me not your musty rules' from the Masque in *Comus* by Thomas Arne, Nocturne in D minor for piano by John Field and 'I have a song to sing' from *The Yeomen of the*

Guard by Arthur Sullivan. The second movement was written for the Aldeburgh Festival 1953 as part of a composite work, *Variations on an Elizabethan Theme,* of which the other five movements were written by Lennox Berkeley, Benjamin Britten, Arthur Oldham, Humphrey Searle and William Walton)

1953-55   *Concerto for Piano and Orchestra*
'To Evelyn Maude'
Commissioned by the City of Birmingham Symphony Orchestra in conjunction with the John Feeney Charitable Trust
First performed by Louis Kentner and the City of Birmingham Symphony Orchestra conducted by Rudolf Schwarz, Town Hall, Birmingham, October 1956

1954   *Four Inventions* for descant and treble recorders
Written for the Society of Recorder Players
First performed by Freda Dinn and Walter Bergmann, Society of Recorder Players' Summer School, Roehampton, July 1954

1955   *Sonata for Four Horns*
First performed by the Dennis Brain Wind Ensemble, Wigmore Hall, December 1955

1956   *Bonny at Morn* Northumbrian Folksong set for unison voices and recorders (two descants and treble)
Written for the 10th birthday of the International Pestalozzi Children's Village at Trogen
(Switzerland)
First performed, April 1956

1956   *Four Songs from the British Isles* for unaccompanied chorus SATB
     1. England: 'Early one morning' 2. Ireland: 'Lilliburlero' 3. Scotland: 'Poortith cauld'
     4. Wales: 'Gwenllian'
Commissioned by the Nordwestdeutschland Sängerbund, Bremen
First performed by the London Bach Group conducted by John Minchinton, Royaumont Festival (France), July 1958

1956-57   *Symphony No. 2*
'To John Minchinton'
Commissioned by the B.B.C.
First performed by the B.B.C. Symphony Orchestra conducted by Sir Adrian Boult, Royal Festival Hall, February 1958

1958   *Crown of the Year* Cantata with text by Christopher Fry for chorus SSA, recorders or flutes, oboe, cornet or trumpet, string quartet, percussion, handbells and piano
Commissioned by Eric Walter White for the centenary celebrations at Badminton School, Bristol
First performed under the composer's direction, July 1958
The instrumental Preludes in this cantata contain settings of 'O Mistress Mine', 'Marlborough s'en va-t-en guerre', the Austrian canon 'O wie wohl ist mir am Abend' and the American folk ballad 'Frankie and Johnny'

1958   *Wadhurst* Hymn Tune (Unto the hills around do I lift up my longing eyes)
Written for the Salvation Army

1958   *Five Negro Spirituals* from *A Child of Our Time* arranged for unaccompanied chorus
1. Steal away 2. Nobody knows 3. Go down, Moses 4. By and by 5. Deep river

1958-61   *King Priam* Opera in 3 acts with text by the composer
'To Karl Hawker'
Written for the Koussevitsky Foundation in memory of Mrs Natalie Koussevitsky
First performed by the Covent Garden Opera conducted by John Pritchard, produced by Sam Wanamaker and with scenery and costumes by Sean Kenny, Coventry Theatre, Coventry, May 1962 (Coventry Cathedral Festival)

1960	*Music* Unison Song (poem by Shelley) for voices, strings and piano, or voices and piano ***Written for the Jubilee of the East Sussex and West Kent Choral Festival 1960*** First performed by the combined choirs of the East Sussex and West Kent Choral Festival conducted by Trevor Harvey, Assembly Hall, Tonbridge Wells, April 1960
1960	*Music for Words Perhaps* Incidental music for speaking voices and chamber ensemble to a sequence of poems by W. B. Yeats ***Commissioned by the B.B.C.*** First broadcast, June 1960
1960	*Lullaby* for six voices, or alto solo (or counter-tenor) and small choir SSTTB (poem by W. B. Yeats) ***Written for the 10th birthday of the Deller Consort*** First performed by the Deller Consort, Victoria and Albert Museum, London, November 1960
1961	*Songs for Achilles* for tenor and guitar with texts by the composer 1. 'In the Tent' 2. 'Across the Plain' 3. 'By the Sea' First performed by Peter Pears and Julian Bream, Aldeburgh Festival, June 1961 (The first song appears in Act 2 of *King Priam*)
1961	*Magnificat and Nunc Dimittis* for chorus SATB and organ (Collegium Sancti Johannis Cantabrigiense) ***Composed for the 450th anniversary of the foundation of St. John's College Cambridge*** 1961 First performed by the St. John's College Chapel Choir conducted by George Guest, March 1962
1962	*Sonata No. 2 for Piano* 'To Margaret Kitchin, with affection and esteem' First performed by Margaret Kitchin, Freemason's Hall, Edinburgh Festival, September 1962 (Motifs from Act 2 of *King Priam* appear in this Sonata)
1962	*Songs for Ariel* for voice and piano (or harpsichord) 1. 'Come unto these yellow sands' 2. 'Full fathom five' 3. 'Where the bee sucks' First performed by Grayston Burgess and Virginia Pleasants at Fenton House, Hampstead, September 1963 (Adapted from incidental music written for a production of Shakespeare's ***The Tempest,*** Old Vic Theatre, London, April 1962. The Songs were arranged in 1964 for an instrumental accompaniment of flute/piccolo, clarinet, horn, percussion ad lib. (bells, bass drum, and harpsichord)
1962	*Praeludium for Brass, Bells and Percussion* ***Commissioned for the 40th anniversary of the B.B.C.*** First performed by B.B.C. Symphony Orchestra conducted by Antal Dorati, Royal Festival Hall, November 1962
1962-63	*Concerto for Orchestra* 'To Benjamin Britten with affection and admiration in the year of his 50th birthday' ***Commissioned for the Edinburgh Festival*** 1963 First performed by the London Symphony Orchestra conducted by Colin Davis, Usher Hall, Edinburgh, August 1963 (Motifs from Acts 2 and 3 of *King Priam* appear in the finale)
1963	*Prelude, Recitative and Aria* for flute, oboe and piano (or harpsichord) First performed by the Oriana Trio on the B.B.C., February 1964 (Arrangement of the third interlude in Act 3 of *King Priam*)
1963-65	*The Vision of Saint Augustine* for baritone solo, chorus and orchestra 'Matri, patrisque in memoriam' ***Commissioned by the B.B.C.*** First performed by Dietrich Fischer-Dieskau and the B.B.C. Symphony Orchestra conducted by the composer at the Royal Festival Hall, January 1966

1965-70	*The Shires Suite* for chorus and orchestra
	This Suite was written during this period for the Leicestershire Schools Symphony Orchestra and consists of the following five movements:—
	Prologue for chorus and orchestra (1965)
	Interlude 1 for orchestra (1970)
	Cantata for chorus and orchestra (1970)
	Interlude 2 for orchestra (1969)
	Epilogue for chorus and orchestra (1965)
	First complete performance by the Schola Cantorum of Oxford and the Leicestershire Schools Symphony Orchestra conducted by the composer, Cheltenham Festival July 1970
1966	*Severn Bridge Variations No. 6 'Braint:*
	Variations on a traditional Welsh melody.
	Commissioned by the B.B.C. West Region
	First performed by the B.B.C. Training Orchestra conducted by Sir Adrian Boult, Brangwyn Hall, Swansea, January 1967.
	(A composite work by Arnold, Hoddinott, Maw, Daniel Jones, Grace Williams, Tippett to commemorate the first birthday of the B.B.C. Training Orchestra, its first visit to Wales, and of the opening of the Severn Bridge.)
1970	*Songs for Dov* for tenor and small orchestra with text by the composer
	'To Eric Walter White'
	Commissioned by the Music Department, University College, Cardiff with assistance from the Welsh Arts Council.
	First performed by Gerald English and the London Sinfonietta conducted by the composer, University College, Cardiff October 1970
	(The first song appears in Act 2 of *The Knot Garden*)
1966-70	*The Knot Garden* opera in 3 acts with text by the composer
	Commissioned by the Royal Opera House, Covent Garden
	'To Sir David Webster of the Royal Opera House, Covent Garden'
	First performed by the Covent Garden Opera conducted by Colin Davis, produced by Peter Hall, designed by Timothy O'Brien and with costumes by Tazeena Firth, Royal Opera House, Covent Garden, December 1970
1970-72	*Symphony No. 3* for Soprano and Orchestra with text by the composer
	'To Howard Hartog'
	Commissioned by the London Symphony Orchestra
	First performed by Heather Harper with the London Symphony Orchestra conducted by Colin Davis, Royal Festival Hall, June 1972
1971	*In Memoriam Magistri* for flute, clarinet and string quartet.
	Commissioned by 'Tempo' magazine in memory of Igor Stravinsky
	First performed by the London Sinfonietta, June 1972
1972-73	*Sonata No. 3 for Piano*
	'To Anna Kallin'
	Commissioned by Paul Crossley
	First performed by Paul Crossley, Bath Festival, May 1973
1973-76	*The Ice Break* opera in 3 acts with text by the composer
	'To Colin Davis'
	Commissioned by the Royal Opera House, Covent Garden
	First performed by Covent Garden Opera, conducted by Colin Davis, produced by Sam Wanamaker, with scenery and costumes by Ralph Koltai, Royal Opera House, Covent Garden, July 1977
1976-77	*Symphony No. 4*
	'To Ian Kemp'
	Commissioned by the Chicago Symphony Orchestra
	First performance by the Chicago Symphony Orchestra conducted by Sir Georg Solti, Chicago, October 1977

Editions
in collaboration with Walter Bergmann

Come Ye Sons of Art Henry Purcell
Ode for the Birthday of Queen Mary (1694) for soli SAAB, chorus SATB and orchestra.

Ode for St Cecilia's Day (1692) Henry Purcell
for soli SAATBB, chorus SATB and orchestra

The Golden Sonata Henry Purcell
for 2 violins and Basso Continuo

Voice and Keyboard Series
Original compositions for one and two voices and figured bass.

Songs
(for high and low voices unless otherwise stated)
J. S. BACH
Amore traditore, Cantata for Bass (Italian, English)
If thou art near & Come sweet death (English, German)
Jesu, in Thy Love, Aria from Cantata 165 for Contralto (English, German)

JOHN BLOW
Tell me no more you love Medium voice
The Selfe Banished

G. F. HANDEL
Lucretia, Cantata for Soprano (Italian, English)

PELHAM HUMFREY
A Hymne to God the Father (words by John Donne)

HENRY PURCELL
Ah, how sweet it is to love
An Epithalamium (Wedding Song)
An Evening Hymn
Bonvica's Song 'O lead me to some peaceful gloom'
Crown the Altar
From rosy bowers
I attempt from love's sickness to fly
If music be the food of love
Let the dreadful engines of eternal will Baritone
Mad Bess
Man is for woman made
Music for a while
Not all my torments
Sweeter than roses
The Blessed Virgin's Expostulation Soprano
The fatal hour comes on
I was within a furlong of Edinborough Town
What shall I do to show how much I love her
When first Amintas sued for a kiss

Duets

JOHN BLOW
Ah Heaven! What is't I hear? Sopranos
If I my Celia could persuade Sopranos

HENRY PURCELL
Elegy upon the Death of Queen Mary (Latin, English) Sopranos
Sound the trumpet Contraltos
There ne'er was so wretched a lover Soprano and Bass
Lost is my quiet Soprano and Bass

I am a composer. That is someone who imagines sounds, creating music from the inner world of the imagination. The ability to experience and communicate this inner world is a gift. Throughout history, society has recognized that certain men possess this gift and has accorded them a special place. But if such men — poets if you like — are honoured, are the products of their imagination of any real value to the society which honours them? Or are we, particularly at this present point in history, deluding ourselves that this may be so?

Like every creative artist, my days are spent pondering, considering, wrestling in my mind with an infinite permutation of possibilities. I must create order out of chaos. The act of imagination is sometimes of great intensity, sometimes more wayward and always, for a big piece of music, prolonged. I am, as it were, possessed, taken over by the creative drive from within, and even when I put away the manuscript paper I find it almost impossible to switch off the inner activity.

I have lived in the country since my student days. This is practical and personal. I need to shut myself away from the noise and activity of the town in order to find some kind of inner silence. The outside world with all its troubles goes on around my personal sanctuary, and I am fully aware of its harsh realities. And I face continually a question within this paradox: has the reality of my imagination any lasting relation to the reality of those events which immediately effect the lives of men?

Concerto in D. for flutes. Oboe. Horns
~~Allegro~~ Allegro non troppo. Andante espressivo. & Strings.
                    Allegro scherzando. Allegro non troppo.

———

Three Songs. 1. Afternoon Tea. 2. Sea Love.
                    3. Arracombe Wood.
Soloist. Eric Shaveson.
          Accompanist - Dora Milner.

———

"Jockey to the Fair".
   Piano Solo. Leslie Orrie. A.R.C.M.
      Grotrian-Steinweg Piano.
          ——— Interval.

      String Quartet in F.
Allegro con brio. Andante espressivo.
Adagio non troppo, con molto sentimento.
   Allegro non troppo, molto leggiero.
          Allegro con brio.
               ~~####~~
   John ~~###~~ Morley   Helen Stewart
   Maurice Hardy.   Mary Gladden.

———

Psalm in C. for chorus & orchestra.
Conductor. David Evans. Mus. Bac.

PROGRAMME.

Concerto in D for Flutes, Oboe, Horns and Strings.

Allegro non troppo.   Andante espressivo.   Allegro scherzando

Allegro non troppo

Three Songs.

1. Afternoon Tea.   2. Sea Love.   3. Arracombe Wood.

Soloist - ERIC SHAXSON.   Accompanist - DORA MILNER.

" Jockey to the Fair."

Piano Solo.   LESLIE ORRIE, A.R.C.M.

Grotrian-Steinweg Piano.

INTERVAL.

String Quartet in F.

Allegro con brio.   Andante Expressivo.

Adagio non troppo, con molto sentimento.

Allegro non troppo, molto leggiero.

Allegro con brio.

JOHN MORLEY.   HELEN STEWART.
MAURICE HARDY.   MARY GLADDEN.

Psalm in C for Chorus and Orchestra.

Conductor: DAVID EVANS, Mus. Bac.

AFTERNOON TEA.

Please you excuse me good five o'clock people,
I've lost my last hatful of words,
And my heart's in the woods up above the
    church steeple,
I'd rather have tea with the birds.
Gay Kate's stolen kisses, poor Barnaby's scars,
Oh, what do they matter, my dear, to the stars,
Or the glow-worms in the lanes.

I'd rather lie under the tall elm trees,
With old rooks talking loud overhead,
To watch a red squirrel run over my knees
Very still on my brackeny bed :
Or wonder what feathers the wrens will be
    taking
For lining their nests next spring,
And why the toss'd shadow of boughs in a
    great wind shaking
Is such a lovely thing.

SEA LOVE.

Tides be runnin' the whole world over,
'Twas only last June month that we
Was thinking the toss and the call in the
    breast of the lover
So everlasting as the sea.

Here's the same little fishes that sputter and
    swim,
And the moon's old glim on the grey wet sand,
And him no more to me nor me to him,
Than the wind goin' over my hand.

ARRACOMBE WOOD.

Some said because he wudn't spaik
Any words to women by yes or no,
Or hold out his hand for parson to shake,
He maun be bird-witted—but I do go
By the lie of the barley which he did sow
And I want no better thing than to hold a rake
Like Dave in his time, or to see him mow.
Put up in Churchyard a month ago,
A bitt'r old soul they said, but it wasn't so ;
His heart was in Arracombe Wood where he
    used to go
To sit and talk with his shadder till sun went
    low ;
Tho' what it was all about us'll never know.
And there baint no mem'ry in the place
Of the old man's footsteps, nor his face,
Arracombe Wood do think more of a crow.

*   *   *   *   *

'Will be violets there in the spring,
In summertime the spider's lace,
And come the fall the whizzle and race
Of the dry dead leaves that the wind gives
    chase ;
And on the eve of Christmas, fallin' snow.

CHARLOTTE MARY MEW.

PSALM.

We have come through the gates of the womb.
Long years we sped that we might clothe
    ourselves in miracles of flesh
And feel and bear and see.
We have felt the wind that sends its crying
    wave
Through cloud and grass and tree.

Thus far we have come, we have won ourselves
    to form.
Girded with dreams we leave the sheltering
    night
And hastening forward, lifted on the storm,
We are brought face to face at last with light.

We have seen the spreading cities and the seas,
The wide pale flood of dawn,
And stared through dark's bright-eyed immen-
    sities.
And watched the grain within its golden cover
In ripeness swelling,
Until at harvest fields were one broad fire
And splendid beyond telling.

There has come this side of the gate the
    evening bird
Filling the woodland with its throbbing calling
    to its mate

Leaf-hidden in the glen.
But for all its singing it cannot cry to God
It cannot pray like men.
All the bells that are ringing from hill to hill,
Voices from furry throats and yellow bill,
The great sea's heaving whisper that began
    so long before the human ear could listen,
These are only sounds that fill our sleep.
A stranger wonder stirs us when we hear the
    voice of man
Speaking his spirit from an upland steep,
His spirit that finds the farthest heavens
    approachable,
And guides the wandering visions of his being
Into a way that winds among bewilderment
Towards a wider seeing.

We have come through the gates ; we are glad
    in our journey.
We challenge with shining eyes the sudden
    stars to swift and dazzling tourney.
And though mist hides the future's massive
    wall,
We see the towering pinnacles of heaven—
We have come—
Our cry goes up and like a sword thrust glides
Through the far reaches of the Empyrean.

Michael Tippett

The concert of works by Michael Tippett, given on Saturday by the Oxted and Limpsfield Players in the Barn Theatre at Oxted, afforded one of those glimpses into the hidden musical activities of this country that gives hope for the future, and are so unwontedly stirring. Of course this sort of thing—compositions by a young composer, performed by friends—is often to be discovered, though not all young musicians have the remarkable gift of Michael Tippett.

The programme was made up of a Concerto for Flutes, Oboe, Horns, and Strings, three songs, pianoforte variations, a string quartet, and a Psalm for chorus and orchestra. Mr. David Evans conducted effectively and with understanding. All the performers were attentive and willing, models of what helpers in the finest causes should be.

Thinking over the bewildering amount of new music with which we were presented, one is struck by the length of Michael Tippett's writing. In one's own student days (he has but just left his) one would, or could, never have written at such length. Fifteen years ago it was all shorter and sharper. Now one is pleased to see that one's successors can be leisurely.

Michael Tippett's manner is modernist, and in the quartet and the Concerto there is the present-day thinning away of material, and deliberate, ruthless, contrapuntal progression of parts. The Psalm must be heard again, and with larger forces, though probably Michael Tippett will prefer to put all behind him and go on to fresh ideas. They will surely be worth it.

Oxted and Limpsfield Players.

DRILL HALL, CATERHAM.

HANDEL'S

"Messiah"

(complete original version),

Soloists, full Choir and Orchestra of 75 Performers

Conductor - Michael Tippett.

Wednesday, 2nd December,

at 7.45 p.m.

Doors Open 7.15.   Cars 10.45.

TICKETS:

2/6 (reserved) ; 1/3 and 7d. (unreserved)

N.B.— 2/6 Seats may be obtained a week in advance from W. J. SNOW,
The Chemist, Caterham.

Only about 60 in audience.

W. & G. GODWIN, PRINTERS, OXTED.

"THE VILLAGE OPERA."

By Mr. Johnson (1729).

Cast :

Sir Nicholas Wiseacre (a Country Gentleman) ...	Leonard A. Moulding
Sir William Freeman (Father to Young Freeman)...	Ernest Hernu
Freeman (otherwise Colin) a Gentleman in the disguise of a gardener, in love with Betty ...	Eric Shaxson
Heartwell (in love with Rosella)	James Lewis
Brush }two roguish Footmen ... ... {	Anthoney Gale
File	Frank Buzzard
Lucas	Albert French
A Steward	John P. Strange
Lady Wiseacre	Robina Bidgood
Rosella (daughter to Sir Nicholas)	Mull Ridge
Betty (Servant to Rosella)	Ouida Ashworth
	Dorothy Shaxson
Susan	

Country Lads and Lasses :

Margaret Mackinnon	Basil Ridley
Doreen Taylor	Raymond Porter
Audrey Davis	Arthur Charman
Josephine Finley	Randolph Robbins
Ursula Webb	Arthur Martin
Kathleen Connell	Fred Everest
Marjorie Dixon	Sidney Parvin
Muriel Fry	Ivor Burton
Dorothy Shaxson	John Buzzard
Nellie Porter	
Ruth Hammond	
Maud Ridley	
Marjorie Streeten	
Lucy Brasier	
Kathleen Freeston	
Mabel Parvin	
Maude Freeston	

Morris Dancers :

John

Harold Dixon, Leslie Ashworth, Albert Faulkner, Evelyn Maude, Charles Rapson, Sodon Bromhead.

Scene :

Act 1. **Scene 1.** The Garden of Sir Nicholas Wiseacre
 Scene 2. A Village Green

INTERVAL.

Act 2. **Scene 1.** The Road before Sir Nicholas's House
 Scene 2. The Garden of Sir Nicholas
 Scene 3. The Same. Midnight

INTERVAL.

Act 3. The Garden of Sir Nicholas

Conductor	... ...	Michael Tippett.
Producer	... ...	Muriel Whitmore
Stage Manager	... ...	Sidney Parvin
Lighting by	... ...	John P. Strange

All Costumes and Stage Settings designed and made by The Oxted and Limpsfield Players.

Orchestra :

1st Violins	Gwendolen Higham, Mary Taylor
2nd Violins	Rose Provis, Betty Parvin
Violas	Margaret Benson-Cooke, Mildred Oliver
'Cellos	Maurice Hardy, Emily McCartney
Flute	Walter Talbot
Oboe	Helen Gaskell
Horn	Frank Probyn
Harpsicord	Freda Ridley
Piano	Evelyn Maude

"THE VILLAGE OPERA."

PERFORMANCE BY OXTED AND LIMPSFIELD PLAYERS.

(FROM OUR SPECIAL CORRESPONDENT.)

OXTED, APRIL 22.

The Village Opera, written by a theatre-poet named Johnson in 1729, which was produced here on Thursday and repeated yesterday at the Barn Theatre, bears a family resemblance to the other entertainments of its kind which sprang up in the successful path of *The Beggar's Opera*. Indeed, this particular specimen so closely resembles *Love in a Village*, which was revived, by a curious coincidence, on the same evening at Hammersmith, that Bickerstaffe must be suspected of having purloined some of Johnson's ideas.

We need do no more in the way of indicating the plot than mention the ingredients, from which the experienced reader may easily compound the familiar intrigue. These are: one crusty country squire (Knight and Justice of the Peace), with comic wife and charming daughter, who is to marry a man she has never seen and who loves another; one young gentleman, apparently a gardener, but in reality the son of another squire (less crusty, but of equal rank with the first), who loves a serving-maid, who likewise is disguised; two rogues, who turn the tables and masquerade as their betters, and so on. In fact, the piece has potentialities of a familiar kind, and when they were turned to good use the entertainment was delightful. The worst mistake was at the beginning, where the young lover had no fewer than nine love-songs, with short scenes or soliloquies between, and, charmingly as Mr. Eric Shaxson sang them, we did want at least to see the lady to whom they were addressed. The most successful scene was that of the elopement, where Mr. Michael Tippett, who arranged and composed the music, showed a real sense of how to handle a dramatic situation in music. The instrumentation in this scene was delightful. But on the whole the music and the performance had too little gaiety in it, and the slow *tempi* at which most things were taken did not make for lightness.

Among the singers Miss Ashworth gave an excellent performance in the "Polly" part of the piece, while Mr. Moulding as the crusty squire and Mr. Anthoney Gale as the chief villain made the most of their humours. Mention must be made of the Morris dance performed by local dancers, which provided a most effective "curtain" for the first act.

QUEEN MARY HALL

(Great Russell Street, W.C.1, near Tottenham Court Road Tube Station)

ENGLISH CHAMBER MUSIC

Friday, November 11th, 1938, at 8.15 p.m.

—

Works by :-

ALAN BUSH
ELIZABETH MACONCHY
MICHAEL TIPPETT

—

Artists :-

BROSA STRING QUARTET

PHYLLIS SELLICK, Piano

ADMISSION - 5/- and 2/6d.

Tickets may be obtained from :- MICHAEL TIPPETT, WHITEGATES COTTAGE, OXTED (Surrey),
or from the Concert Secretary, QUEEN MARY HALL, Great Russell Street, London, W.C.1

ENGLISH CHAMBER MUSIC *S. Manch*

Four modern works, three string quartets and a new pianoforte sonata, by young English composers were played at Queen Mary Hall on Friday night. The Brosa Quartet gave a good account of Alan Bush's " Dialectic " and Elizabeth Maconchy's Second Quartet, which are alike in that they pursue a train of thought with vigorous logic but differ in that Bush does it drily and Maconchy with passion. A string quartet by Michael Tippett had a finale written on the same lines—set a pattern going, pursue it in four parts and see what comes of it. But it also had a slow movement of sustained lyrical feeling, which is rare in these days. The harmonic-melodic style of this movement did not quite fit the logico-contrapuntal manner of the other movements, but it is a work of great promise and of some value. The same composer's piano sonata, played with a quick grasp of all its points by Miss Phyllis Sellick, was, however, a more assured accomplishment. Here is someone who did not insult the piano either by treating it as an overgrown dulcimer in the modern manner or by writing merely pianistic music as virtuosos do. Here was music for the piano that was real music and was at the same time conceived in terms of the medium. Mr. Tippett's ancestry may be sought in Beethoven ; at any rate his music has Beethoven's quality of being thoughtful and still remaining in love with the instruments of its execution instead of hating or despising them as many modern composers appear to do.

here
follows page 2

S. Maude.

THE

ROYAL COLLEGE OF MUSIC

PATRONS—
HIS MAJESTY THE KING
HER MAJESTY THE QUEEN
PRESIDENT—H.R.H. THE PRINCE OF WALES, K.G.
DIRECTOR—SIR HUGH P. ALLEN, K.C.V.O., M.A., D.MUS., D.LITT.

Royal College of Music Patron's Fund

(Founded by LORD PALMER, F.R.C.M.)

ORCHESTRAL REHEARSAL

At the Royal College of Music, Prince Consort Road, S.W. 7

CONDUCTOR :
DR. MALCOLM SARGENT, F.R.C.M.

FRIDAY, 12th JULY, 1935, at 10 a.m.

(FOR COMPOSERS)

1. SYMPHONY for Orchestra, in B flat ... *Michael Tippett*
(First movement)
Conducted by THE COMPOSER

*2. CHINESE BALLET ... Lady Yang ... *Lois Henderson*

*3. POLKA for Violoncello and Orchestra ... *David Evans*
Violoncello : MAURICE HARDY

*4. PRELUDE for Orchestra ... ... *S. D. Elliott*

*5. RECITATIVE and DANCE for Orchestra ... *William L. Reed*

From 10 till about 11-50 will be devoted to rehearsal ;
at about 12 the works will be played straight through.

* First performance.

THE LONDON SYMPHONY ORCHESTRA

R.C.M. PATRON'S FUND
S. Maude 1935

NEW ORCHESTRAL WORKS

The last of the series of morning rehearsals was given by the London Symphony Orchestra under Dr. Sargent's direction in the concert hall of the Royal College of Music yesterday.

Five orchestral works by young, and it may be hoped, rising composers were brought forward. The most significant of them, the first movement of a Symphony in B flat, was conducted by its composer, Michael Tippett. Its significance is that the composer attempts to weld together strongly contrasted moods into a consistent design. The opening *Lento* arouses interest, not completely sustained throughout, perhaps, but it is to be remembered that this movement is intended to be followed by others which may justify its preludial character. The actual themes seem too small for the emphasis laid on them, and some of the *fortissimo* emphasis seemed needlessly crude. But it is the crudeness of over-earnest youth, not of ineptitude.

MR. WALTER GOEHR'S CONCERT ? 1943

MICHAEL TIPPETT'S NEW WORK

Mr. Walter Goehr can be relied on to go off the beaten track for his programmes. For his Saturday concert at Wigmore Hall his taste fell on nice light things that were no strain on the attention on a July afternoon, although he included one new work, a concerto for double string orchestra by Michael Tippett.

This proved to be a well knit, skilfully contrived composition, in which intricacy of detail in rhythm and texture was made to serve the ends of a larger design. The quick movements were energetic without being restless and the slow movement, though astringent and not very lyrical, still expressed something more contemplative. The whole was a successful essay in music as both thought and pattern.

The programme began and ended with French pieces. In between came Haydn's trumpet concerto and five of Wolf's songs with orchestra. The concerto, being late Haydn, is attractive to listen to and interesting as writing for the instrument of that day. Mr. George Eskdale's attempt to treat the solo part as a flexible soprano melodic line was not altogether successful because his *tempo rubato* disturbed the rhythm. Nor are Wolf's songs an unqualified success with orchestral accompaniment, although the composer himself had a hand in some of the transcriptions. The intimacy of the connexion between voice and piano is lost and the element of suggestion in which the piano excels is weakened by the positive colours of the orchestra.

Mr. Victor Carne brought a pleasing tenor voice and an intimate style to the singing of the songs. The fact that the interpretation in these two cases was not fully effective detracted very little from the interest of the works or from the pleasure of hearing them presented by Mr. Goehr's efficient little orchestra and the capable soloists.

FIFTH CONCERT

YOUNG BRITISH COMPOSERS

ARNOLD van WYK:
Three Improvisations on Dutch Folk songs
for Piano Duet
Howard Ferguson   -   -   -   Denis Mathews

AUBREY BOWMAN:
Four Songs for Baritone and Piano
First Performance
. . . " And the Spring remains " - Lament and Triumph -
Thompson's Last Stand   -   Song of the Night Market
Laurence Holmes   -   -   -   Howard Ferguson

BERNARD STEVENS:
Trio for Piano, Violin and 'Cello
First Performance
Eiluned Davies, piano   -   *Olive Zorian*, violin
Norina Semino, 'cello

NOEL MEWTON-WOOD:
Trio for Violin, Viola and 'Cello
First Performance
Olive Zorian, violin - *Winifred Copperwheat*, viola
Norina Semino, 'cello

MICHAEL TIPPETT:
Second String Quartet
First Performance
The Olive Zorian String Quartet

Saturday, March 27th, 1943
at 2.30 p.m.

WORKS BY YOUNG COMPOSERS

The Boosey and Hawkes concert of new works of young British composers given at the Wigmore Hall yesterday was on the whole disappointing.

Although Bernard Stevens's piano trio is a profounder piece of writing than Noel Mewton-Wood's string trio, both works proved to be little more than competent essays in note spinning.

The really bright spot in the programme was Michael Tippett's second string quartet. It is the work of an alert and imaginative mind, whose individual approach to the problem of form, intense feeling for rhythm, and keen melodic sense are extraordinarily impressive.   5 March   R. H.

WAR TROUBLES DO NOT DAUNT THIS CHOIR

The sound of the final chorus from a cantata by Bach sung at Morley College on Saturday night was ravishing. It made it almost impossible to realise that owing to the illness of a soloist the programme had been changed at the last moment.

Nor was it easy to remember that this admirable organisation has much difficulty in keeping going, what with the scarcity of singers and players as well as the hindrances threatened by outside authorities.

After the Bach chorus the return to a modern idiom might well have been distressing. But Michael Tippett's Second String Quartette which followed is not only good to hear and to think about but has a slow movement as exquisite as anything heard during the evening.

This work, which is altogether notable, was well played by the Zorian Quartette.   Scott Goddard

Music

By WILLIAM GLOCK

A NEW composer has emerged in English music. All I know so far of Michael Tippett's is the piano sonata* of 1938 and the 2nd string quartet of 1942; but these will serve as adequate background, I think, for a few words on his style and possible significance.

We now recognise Benjamin Britten as a different kind of composer from any of his English predecessors. The reason is partly that he has not been influenced at all by the first generation of modern French composers; that his features are clear from the pockmarks of enthusiasm for Sibelius; and that he has never projected on to the contemporary screen a Brahms worn out with endless re-showing. Tippett brings an equal gust of fresh air, though he can survey the lushness of many of his seniors and still write *dolce cantabile*, and can recognise the "outer darkness of Brahms" (as Arnold Bax calls it in his recent autobiography) but still use the world of the Paganini Variations for the first movement of his piano sonata.

Exploration

Britten absorbs the music of the past whenever it is close to him in spirit. Tippett, on the other hand, explores deliberately from Pérotin to Hindemith and from plainsong to jazz and negro spirituals. Thus in the 2nd quartet he uses madrigal technique for the first movement, fugue for the second, formal repetitions and jazz for the scherzo, and what he calls the "Beethoven-traditional drama" for the finale. The piano sonata has an equal range of style and an equal unity. In both works, I think, the first and third movements are the most important: they contain what is essentially original in Tippett's music.

What is this originality? First and foremost, it is a new sense of rhythm gained chiefly from a new relationship with music outside the Viennese period and all that can be connected with it. The first movement of the piano sonata is studded with formidable time signatures: ⅜ plus ⅝ is quite typical; yet the result is perfectly natural because every factor in the music conspires towards the same end. To regularise the barlines would be to reduce the composer's intentions to nonsense. The freedom is for the ear and not merely for the eye. Together with the buoyant and thrusting rhythm, both here and in the string quartet, is an extreme simplicity of melodic line and (especially in the sonata) of harmonic progression. And since it is music and not fabrication, such simplicity makes its direct impression. Both works, indeed, lack any trace of psychological complexity. They express unrestricted pleasure in using new techniques rather than in conveying some personal doctrine.

Sense of Tradition

Both Aaron Copland, in "Modern Music," and Osbert Sitwell (in the March number of "Horizon") have been reminding us that the period between the two wars produced a succession of masterpieces in the various arts which we shall do well to rival in the next twenty years. I doubt very much whether, in music at least, we *shall* rival the best works of the "interbellum." But what we have a right to expect is a decision as to the *kind* of music that will come in the next period of maturity; and Tippett's contribution, I feel certain, will not be negligible. I have insisted often enough on the need for a wider outlook on the past. In Tippett's music you will find an embodiment of this sense of tradition.

Meanwhile, I suggest that such pianists as Clifford Curzon, Kendall Taylor, Denis Matthews, and Noel Mewton-Wood should play the sonata regularly; and that our best quartets should study Tippett No. 2.

* Published by Schott and Co. records by Rymington van Wyck.

MICHAEL TIPPETT SENT TO PRISON

DR. VAUGHAN WILLIAMS'S PLEA FOR COMPOSER

MICHAEL KEMP TIPPETT, 38, director of music at Morley College since 1940, whose compositions were described by Dr. Vaughan Williams as forming "a distinct national asset," was at Oxted, Surrey, yesterday, sentenced to three months' imprisonment for failing to comply with the conditions of his registration as a conscientious objector.

Mr. Howe Pringle, prosecuting, said that the appellant tribunal decided in May last year that Tippett should take up full-time A.R.P., N.F.S., or farm work. He was directed into farm work but failed to comply with the directions. When interviewed in April, he stated that his views were such that he did not feel he could comply with the conditions.

Dr. Ralph Vaughan Williams, called for the defence, said, " I think Tippett's pacifist views entirely wrong, but I respect him very much for holding them so firmly. I think his compositions are very remarkable, and form a distinct national asset, and will increase the prestige of this country in the world. As regards his teachings at Morley College, it is distinctly work of national importance to create a musical atmosphere at the college and elsewhere. We know music is forming a great part in national life now; more since the war than ever before, and everyone able to help on with that work is doing work of national importance."

Mrs. E. Hubback, principal of Morley College, said that she had always known Tippett as a pacifist and was convinced of his entire sincerity.

My generation was the same age as the century. I was born in 1905, lived in the depths of an unpolluted countryside and remained ignorant and innocent of all events outside the family until the start of the Great War. As the men marched away I remember the sense of their lighthearted confidence, singing those songs that gave me my first musical excitement. I was so young still that I could reduce the significance of the war to those songs. When the war ended, the springtime of my life coincided with the momentary springtime all Europe felt as the killing stopped. In 1923 I came to London as a student of eighteen. I now knew that my life lay in artistic creation. I had no misgivings whatsoever. I scarcely considered any of the great contemporary events which seemed to lie outside my musical needs, concerned only with the huge ferment of artistic creation of the period and the general mood — in England at any rate — of frenetic gaiety.

Into this nonchalant atmosphere there began to dawn the first truths about the war, and strangely enough this experience happened to me when I went to see the film *The Four Horsemen of the Apocalypse.* This was popular art. We all went to see Valentino in his latest movie. In fact I can recall nothing of the love story, all I remember is the violence and destruction of the war sequences. And what I never forgot was the extraordinary image of four horsemen flying across the screen at every moment of destruction, and the doom-laden sound of Beethoven's 'Coriolan' Overture. These things combined to give me the sense that there were enormous forces beyond human control which could simply destroy the whole fabric of our civilization. At the end of the film came the first pictures I had ever seen of the Flanders graveyards: row upon row of little white crosses. This gave me the horrified understanding that so many thousands of young men whom I had seen marching lightheartedly away, had ended under the earth. I burst into tears (virtually) and went out. I realized that although I was still a very young man and had a great deal to learn about the merely technical questions of music and was going to immerse myself in everything to do with the technique of my art, that this was something which I simply could not forget: there was a necessity for art of our time in some way, when it had learned its own techniques, to be concerned with what was happening to this 'apocalyptic' side of our present time.

What indeed was happening to all of us of my age in England, was a realization that the spring was false, and that in fact it was still winter. For the majority of my countrymen perhaps there had never been a spring at all. With this realization every artist of my generation became politically involved in some way or other. I remember how I went up North in 1932 to a work-camp, helping unemployed ironstone miners, then hiked into the coalfields and saw for the first time, with horrified eyes, the undernourished children. When I returned to the well-fed South, I was ashamed.

I saw now, and understood for the first time, the stark realities of human life for so many people and accepted the overwhelming need for compassion with regard to such things. So I was faced, consciously perhaps for the first time, with the fundamental question: had I the right to turn away from such reality, to shut myself up to write abstract music? I could have said music is something so disrelated to this reality that everybody must go out and take political or philanthropic action in order to have some immediate impact upon the situation. Every artist was faced with this at that time as they have perhaps always been. It was a real dilemma and it was not solved by a moral determination to know which was which, but by the fact that the actual drive of one's needs as an artist was so great that it forced me back to the studio for the purpose of writing music, although I was quite certain somewhere that at some point, music could have a direct relation also to the compassion that was so deep in my own heart.

There were other huge political forces on the boil. Not only socialism but fascism. With the meteoric rise of Hitler, a kind of mad irrationality appeared in Europe, so truly evil that few of us had any experience to understand it. The whole Jewish race was to be systematically liquidated it appeared.

Although the artist appears to be locked away, doing his particular thing, one could not, at that time, but be aware of what was going on. I was almost peculiarly aware. I was drawn by something of my own entrails into what was happening, particularly in Germany. The Jews were the particular scape-goats of everything, for every kind of standing outcast, whether in Russia or America or even in England. For these people I knew somehow I had to sing songs. Suddenly, in fact the day after war broke out, the whole thing welled up in me in a way which I can remember exactly. I simply had to go and begin to write *A Child of Our Time*. I felt I had to express collective feelings and that could only be done by collective tunes such as the Negro spirituals, for these tunes contain a deposit of generations of common experience.

As the preparations for war began in earnest, I watched but did not take part. I knew that something was forcing me to be a Conscientious Objector. For failing to carry out my conditions of exemption I was given a prison sentence and was locked away in Wormwood Scrubs. I was now myself an outcast. It seemed indeed that this particular split between myself and society was part of the continuous and wider split between the artist affirming what he believes to be absolute values, and society which seemed bent on destroying itself. The climax of my sense of isolation came shortly afterwards when the noble Christian allies decided to put their faith in that masterpiece of technics — the atom bomb. Simultaneously, the concentration camps were opened. I found in these obscenities, as did many others, a most violent and enduring shock to my sense of what humanity might be at all. A denial of any and every affirmation which the poet might make, whether in the name of God or of Mankind. What price Beethoven now?

© Michael Tippett: excerpt from *Moving Into Aquarius* published by Paladin Books, and reproduced by kind permission.

In replying to this letter, please write on the envelope:—

Number _5832_ Name _M. K. Tippett_ 21/6/23

............WORMWOOD SCRUBB...... Prison

The following regulations as to communications, by Visit or Letter, between prisoners and their friends are notified for the information of their correspondents.

The permission to write and receive letters is given to prisoners for the purpose of enabling them to keep up a connection with their respectable friends.

All letters are read by the Prison Authorities. They must be legibly written and not crossed. Any which are of an objectionable tendency, either to or from prisoners, will be suppressed.

Prisoners are permitted to receive and to write a letter at intervals, which depend on the rules of the stage they attain by industry and good conduct; but matters of special importance to a prisoner may be communicated at any time by letter (prepaid) to the Governor, who will inform the prisoner thereof, if expedient.

In case of misconduct, the privilege of receiving and writing a letter may be forfeited for a time.

Money, Postage Stamps, Food, Tobacco, Clothes, etc., should not be sent to prisoners for their use in Prison, as nothing is allowed to be received at the Prison for that purpose.

Persons attempting to communicate with prisoners contrary to the rules, or to introduce any article to or for prisoners, are liable to fine or imprisonment, and any prisoner concerned in such practices is liable to be severely punished.

Prisoners' friends are sometimes applied to by unauthorised persons, to give or send money, under pretence that it will be for the benefit of the prisoners. The people who make these requests are trying to get money for themselves by fraudulent pretences. If the friends of a prisoner are asked for money, either verbally or by letter, they should at once inform the Governor of the Prison about the matter, and send him any letter they have received.

Prisoners are allowed to receive visits from their friends, according to rules, at intervals which depend on their stage.

When visits are due to prisoners, notification will be sent to the friends whom they desire to visit them.

No. 243 (15717—19-4-23)

Evelyn dear – no letters allowed EXCEPT an answer to each one I send out – every fortnight. Write V.W. if you will & thank him from me. If the Surrey Mirror has a write-up of his evidence let John have a copy to show Scholtz, Boult etc. Ring Ellick & wish her luck for Sat & July 4. Tell John to wish Tony luck for his Prom July 7. As Bennet will contribute to the case if you write. Tell John to get the message about Eric Mason's Appellate from Peter. &½ tell him & Ben to give their recital to us as soon as possible. Send a message of encouragement to the good Rose. Visitors will be in a month. Would like to see John & tha. I suppose Ben & Tony would talk same language. If not David, Fresca, Ben, you? As to holiday – it seems I shall be out Aug 21st all being well – early morning. If John can wait I suppose it would be nice to have a week in Cornwall with the 'children', & possibly some time with David after. Otherwise shall be rampaging to get back to work. It'll be a desire to be with one's own again & 'praps a need for fresh air. Please send me in as books. Art of Fuge (on the piano), War & Peace – any good work on Astrology – the Cornford etc – 2 or so at a time the sooner the better. I think I can have up to four at once – but I'll let you know how it goes next letter. They remain in the prison library. Shall want if possible 3 or 4 more Gillette shape razor-blades. My father would spare some I think. Came from Oxted chained to the young soldier whose case we heard first, & with one of the lads who stole the rabbits. Wasn't that curious? It's rather like the first days of term before the days began to move. In the good mood it's rejoicing it is – as you can tell everyone – comradeship, peace & a full heart. On the recoil it's somewhat of a noise & negative & like being unwell in a foreign hotel.

On second thoughts tell John as to the various plans suggested at Eric Mason's Appellate etc that they're better left – & in general not to worry about me – this includes the visit of Mrs Mason. John will understand, & tell him straight away. It is only gradually that one takes on the new life. Write straight away if you can & I'll get it quickly then.

Tomorrow is Quaker meeting which I look forward to. There's also a brass orchestra I hope to be allowed some time to help on & keep on it going. Love. Michael.

In replying to this letter, please write on the envelope:—

5/7/-

Number ......*5834*..... Name ....*M. Tuppett*...

.... Prison

The following regulations as to communications, by Visit or Letter, between prisoners and their friends are notified for the information of their correspondents.

The permission to write and receive letters is given to prisoners for the purpose of enabling them to keep up a connection with their respectable friends.

All letters are read by the Prison Authorities. They must be legibly written and not crossed. Any which are of an objectionable tendency, either to or from prisoners, will be suppressed.

Prisoners are permitted to receive and to write a letter at intervals, which depend on the rules of the stage they attain by industry and good conduct; but matters of special importance to a prisoner may be communicated at any time by letter (prepaid) to the Governor, who will inform the prisoner thereof, if expedient.

In case of misconduct, the privilege of receiving and writing a letter may be forfeited for a time.

Money, Postage Stamps, Food, Tobacco, Clothes, etc., should not be sent to prisoners for their use in Prison, as nothing is allowed to be received at the Prison for that purpose.

Persons attempting to communicate with prisoners contrary to the rules, or to introduce any article to or for prisoners, are liable to fine or imprisonment, and any prisoner concerned in such practices is liable to be severely punished.

Prisoners' friends are sometimes applied to by unauthorised persons, to give or send money, under pretence that it will be for the benefit of the prisoners. The people who make these requests are trying to get money for themselves by fraudulent pretences. If the friends of a prisoner are asked for money, either verbally or by letter, they should at once inform the Governor of the Prison about the matter, and send him any letter they have received.

Prisoners are allowed to receive visits from their friends, according to rules, at intervals which depend on their stage.

When visits are due to prisoners, notification will be sent to the friends whom they desire to visit them.

No. 243 (15717—19 4-23)

42

Evelyn dear. Y'r letter was a great pleasure to get. I will reply to its contents first. Books – I got the 2 devotional books, but haven't yet read them. In fact I read little. Cell task occupies a lot of time, & there is a baby prisoners orchestra here wh I conduct & try to improve – & that takes 2 hours out of possible reading time. It's a sort of light café orchestra, & with instruments all of different pitch – in fact throw-outs. But we manage. & I hope to get in better music. On Sunday we are to play in chapel, in the middle of a recital by Peter Pears & Ben Britten – all v. amusing. So don't worry to chase after books. But there is a text-book I'd like (I've got the Bach) – will you ring Alec Robertson & ask from me if he cld spare me a copy of his book: The Problem of Plainsong – on the art of wh he is an authority. If & when you get it take it to Friends House as you did the Bach. I shld n't send the Cornford just yet. / Tell Mother if you're writing any time not to wonder at the letters about me to her – I'm sort of a general favourite. As to getting down there, I might manage after the proper holiday, on way back from Cornwall if it's to be there – otherwise I think to write the long-delayed 1st movement of the old 4tet & then take another break away, at Exmouth p'raps, & then start the Symphony – wh will be a big thing. / I agree with you completely abt press hoo-ha – no interested party shld write at all. / Holiday – I'm quite as ready to g. with David first. The point is anyhow that I come out Sat. 21st Aug. & will make the 4tet performance at Wigmore the public meeting ground for all & Sunday. Rose choirs etc – then come home & get things together etc, Sunday. / The question of my getting something from people like books is difficult. I don't know for instance how much I really get from David – sometimes I'm rather repressed by him. I get a great deal from you – but that is a more subtle business, & in this case must wait till I'm properly home & at work again. / Keep the Hölderlin Maritain etc – they're for my library & the autumn. / Haven't read any Paul yet. It hasn't worked out quite as I expected. One gets not only fallow but sluggish. We're all the same. You can't manufacture the proper conditions & here is a lot of internal strain – a great deal of dreaming & inner adjustment – & the weeks inside seem monstrously lengthy & disproportionate so that you fail to realise how easily they pass to those outside or how little one might oneself get done outside. / As far as

I know there is nothing against length in letters in. Write on their paper perhaps. You might send some 18 or 20 stave score - a few sheets - with the Robertson book. I shall probably get permission to use it. But 12 stave will do, if the other is too big.

And now messages: a special one this time to Ben & Miriam, who are after all my house & my own. Tell Miriam to use the tin of sugar in the larder which Den gave me, for jam. I shall have forgotten the taste by the time I come out. I have already. Is anyone in the cottage yet?

A message of greeting to the choirs 1st (book under T.). Hope they're managing. Write if you will to the deputy Tanner - & say he must choose music to suit himself - & that I shall probably take at least September clear away for my own work - (if not give the choir up altogether).

Ask to pay for those times he deputised for whom I signed the register - & generally to try & solve the payments, claims problems of that choir, via the Sec. of the W.E.A. It is done terminally, & so quite soon. 2nd Tooting (under T.) Just send them greetings, either via Tony or the Sec. Will see them again next term of course / Morley. Give them best wishes for the concert on the 17th, & hope they do well. Will be thinking of them. You can let them know sometime that I shall make my first reappearance on 21st Aug at Wigmore. / Fresca: Give her my love - tell her I'm managing fine - that I came across a typical Irish ABBA tune in Songs of Praise masquerading as English Traditional Melody.

If she thinks to come to the 4 Act on the 21st, would like to lunch with her beforehand, & so with. / If this gets you in time ring Peter & Ben, Primrose 5826 & wish Ben well for his Prom on Sat evening - & tell them not to be distressed by the 'orchestra' in Handel's 'Largo' & Bach's Chorale on Sunday. Its for the sake of social progressiveness not to rival their artistry. If they're still at home on the 21st would like to breakfast with them & both. / John Amis: Not to forget 6 tickets for Tooting choir via Tony for 17th - & if to spare send a couple to Wilf Franks, c/o 45 Holmesdale Rd, N.6. To send my love to the two Walters: to Goehr, not to worry abt the 17th, but that he'll probably gain all the publicity - & good luck to him etc. To Bergmann my love - & could he possibly begin to look at the printed church music of Wedhes for Morley next session - I think "Absolom, my son," or some such title a v. fine one. To Schotts in general, Cheminant & Steffens my regards & good wishes

John can do all that. As to visit: the order is due on Nov 19th, but it probably wont reach John till 21st or 22nd. It will have 3 names on it: his, Tony's & Brittens (?) – is that OK? otherwise we must invent. All the 3 come together – 2.30 at the prison is a good time. You take a no 7 bus from Oxford Circus to the door (½ an hour) or Central London to Wood Lane, 1½d Trolley bus a minute or two to Du Cane Avenue & walk down 2 or 300 yds. Quite quick. Ring the bell & ask to see me & show the order. Shd like to see & read & use any press notices etc.

As to the new 4th! movement (please keep these notes): I think the 2nd subject needs a longish bit (B) & the repeat of A to lead straight to the constricted portion: probably by using some of the old material of the & reach the same clow before cello up-going cadenza as before – then a possibly contrapuntal development of wot the reprise of the opening themes will form the climax – & a recapitulation as varied as the material allows & leading by the same coda material to the down-going cello cadenza.

So far I've only had this one 'thought' about my music, as above: I dont think its any good trying to make things move when the circumstances forbid any real 'output' or creation. Prison is not a creative experience at any point – except perhaps in human contacts. I dare say it will seem less wasteful when one looks back – perhaps it may be a real holiday, mentally. Its difficult inside not to give exaggerated importance to its actual length of days – & to brood on them so that they go slower. In fact I am pretty active & the time passes somehow. [not with yr answer.]

Razor blades we are allowed to change the permitted one each week. I have it only in 'property' – if you post some more to me, they'll just be put with the rest & I can either use them or bring them home. I like to keep shaven & as clean as maybe. Its better for one's self-respect. Any blades that fit a Gillette. 3-hole type – or slots. / I've experienced a lucky chance with eye-exercises that may be helpful afterwards. Its v. hard on the eyes here. Sewing etc, & a bad light in the cell & little time to exercise at all. I shall just about manage to keep them no worse than they are.

One has moments of nostalgia, but not too many. I shall come through. Its boring of course. It is good to know things happen outside.

Much love to all friends – & specially to you. Michael

I dreamed of a green flowering olive tree in spring, last night. Good.

In replying to this letter, please write on the envelope:—

Number _5832._   Name _Teffett M._ *19/4*

.... Prison

The following regulations as to communications, by Visit or Letter, between prisoners and their friends are notified for the information of their correspondents.

The permission to write and receive letters is given to prisoners for the purpose of enabling them to keep up a connection with their respectable friends.

All letters are read by the Prison Authorities. They must be legibly written and not crossed. Any which are of an objectionable tendency, either to or from prisoners, will be suppressed.

Prisoners are permitted to receive and to write a letter at intervals, which depend on the rules of the stage they attain by industry and good conduct; but matters of special importance to a prisoner may be communicated at any time by letter (prepaid) to the Governor, who will inform the prisoner thereof, if expedient.

In case of misconduct, the privilege of receiving and writing a letter may be forfeited for a time.

Money, Postage Stamps, Food, Tobacco, Clothes, etc., should not be sent to prisoners for their use in Prison, as nothing is allowed to be received at the Prison for that purpose.

Persons attempting to communicate with prisoners contrary to the rules, or to introduce any article to or for prisoners, are liable to fine or imprisonment, and any prisoner concerned in such practices is liable to be severely punished.

Prisoners' friends are sometimes applied to by unauthorised persons, to give or send money, under pretence that it will be for the benefit of the prisoners. The people who make these requests are trying to get money for themselves by fraudulent pretences. If the friends of a prisoner are asked for money, either verbally or by letter, they should at once inform the Governor of the Prison about the matter, and send him any letter they have received.

Prisoners are allowed to receive visits from their friends, according to rules, at intervals which depend on their stage.

When visits are due to prisoners, notification will be sent to the friends whom they desire to visit them.

No. 243 (15717—19 4-23)

Evelyn dearest. have been hurrying up my cell task so as to be able to write at leisure. I sent off the visiting order with the one envelope, so this may be delayed while I get hold of another. I'd better answer yr letter first. / Tell Morley if still going that I got their messages & thought of them hard at 6 p.m. last Saturday. And will you ask Miss Cowles there what the date of next term is - because it may curtail the holiday away to 10 days. I'll come back on this. / Please write Rouse - say I am so glad to hear he's written; will look forward to reading the letter when I come out. Sorry he's been ill again. Tell him plans to be at Portloe & shall I look him up on way back. Does he know off-hand a pub, hotel, that wld breakfast the 5 of us on Sunday, 22nd, at St Austell. When I come to holiday you'll understand why. / Betty Hamilton leave/- d° the green woods. & others - but tell John Allen if you think fit where I am obtainable when I'm out. /

Holiday: I'll write it you tho' I intend to ask John to do the trains etc on visit. But you can never be sure of anything in prison! If the Sat. night train is OK, we go to St Austell & bus to Mevagissey - John must check the Sunday buses: we need to be at Mevagissey by lunch time (I believe it gets in at 1.30 or so) & therefore take food for him: & walk along the coast to Portloe getting in to tea: tho' it is a poor step. If this won't work we must go to Truro & walk over Malpas ferry & Lamorran woods. J. needs to get £10 out of Britten(?) in cash for me: get tickets for Ben & myself & let me have the change. The ration book etc I wld have to get you to do & send after me. It may be rather rash to plan so hasty a departure: but it feels good. I'm hoping that a day's good food will recover me: I'm as weak as a kitten: & we shall have to carry packs. If John has no pack he can ~~have~~ share mine: or have you a Berghen of Evans? I don't see how I can be away more than 2 weeks at the most because of the fanfare for the church. If Morley first do is Thurs 2nd Sept. then I'd better be back for it & so home. We'd better settle this I won't David. I suggest you advise Walter of the fanfare commission, & that I will come 1 night to Exmouth to see them, or 2 if possible: & put off the real visit to October. It wld be advisable therefore for D. & Laxoma to be away already so that I can go there on Monday the 30th. But it won't be for long if Morley is open. Otherwise I wld like to get home by Sat. 4th for certain. If Rouse suggests that we all breakfast with him, then I cld cut a visit there on the return & travel to David on the Sunday. But if Morley is not opening till the 6th Sept, then I'd enjoy a night at Rouse's, Sun 29, some days with D. & L. & 2 nights at Exmouth & travel home morning train Sat. I'll write you next time the clothes

47

I wld want in the pack - apart from a pair of flannels & a jacket to replace the suit I've got here, & will wear at the Wigmore. I think, by the way, it might be worth putting a nicely worded advert. in P.N. for the Aug 14th issue, that I am coming out all being well, & hope to be present at W.H. at the perf. of the 2nd 4tet. In order to do Cooper a possible fillip for his concert. Or is this too publicity like? I think actually the C.B.C.o. wld put it in under their notes. It's right, in any case to make it an occasion of public return, so that the more that broadcast around the better. / Tell mother also that I'm so glad to hear of my nephew John's successful operations. / Comfort me a bone I meant to buy so don't worry. Will be glad of the Robertson I think. Ring him & thank him if you will, & give him a cheerful message from me: he's a very nice chap. / If you have time write a note to Emily Borne, Fred Mayo's sister, & give her a kind message, & say I'm so glad to hear Fred is joining the hospital staff. Hope to see her at W.H. on 21st. / When writing to mother tell her I wrote Phyl before I came in, but no reply. / What you wrote abt "endless patches of Time" was extraordinarily helpful. I do believe in it, & it gives strength to endure the apparent wastage. (Incidentally the Symphony is gestating alright, almost consciously. I shall have the whole form worked out in my mind, by the time I come out. It's going to be a big thing.) I am only really close to you, B.B. & John Amis - no one else. And while John is simply a projection of my musical self & therefore often in my mind, Ben is v. near, just because he is himself. I sense, so moved by my imprisonment? for, of course, one's something almost eternal!! & the aloneness is more to be expected. Everyone else is perhaps the concert here was a terrific success & to hear him at the piano was absurdly deep-going. The orchestra did not function. I'll tell you all the story sometime. I haven't been to practise this week either. It matters not, except where I can be of service. The 'library' is musical comedy selections & v. tiring. Later this week I go on 'association' as it is called, & have meals at tables in community, & move to another cell - the Upper School! & that marks my exact half-way, wh will seem better afterwards I think. / Cld you get me a fresh tin of Calvert's tooth-powder, & send in for me. / I have my specs in fact. But the truth is that the strain of the eyes is v. great, & I shall have to do exercises in all seriousness this autumn to try & undo the damage. / You might suggest to Fresca, if she is still at Mill House, that she bottles a few things, extra, for me. I shall be sorely in need of that sort of food, at suppers & so on. & generally the Allisons have quantities. I want to try & get a better supper arrangement for it anyhow, to try & feed myself up - I'm v. thin & bony - if not haggard! / Fresca has the Irish full-Sunday Journals. / Wld like you to cheer Steffens up if you see a way. I can't help feeling that wrongly or rightly, the publicity has done good not only to the cause but like music – & he need have no fear. And please write Mayo – 24, L.t. H. Strecker, c/o Schotts – & give him my love & good wishes & tell him I'm going to surviving & working on a smashing symphony: & give him news of the various nice things said by V.W. etc / Wd like you to ask Rose if she managed to get any of Cooper's handbills for 7th & 21st to send out – & to get them via John if not. / You will let me know facewise abt Pam's new babe, when? & what sex? & name? & please abt Gillian. / You know the thought of you being whisked to Oxford is somewhat shattering. I can't quite imagine what becomes of the cottage without you nearby. I am not in the least ready for such an eventuality – oh dear. But we must cross the bridge before we reach it. / Wish I cd have seen the ceanothus & the jasmine. But will next year. What they want if you can manage – is good earth fetched to them from elsewhere because they are really bedded on the clay foundations of the house & with no proper soil except what is brought them. I'm sure he'd do it if you explain. / The MS. has come, but I haven't applied to have it yet. I just won't went all on the Symphony – & have the plan for the future. Wd like to know the exact date proposed, if you cd ask Benj. If I apply to get my next visit (due in my last week) put ahead, wd it amuse you to come & see me in my prison clothes &I'll send the letter to mother say. & This must not interfere with meeting me at 7.30 on the day. So d'better come & breakfast at Ben's too.) It wont be worth seeing the others & myself, as I shall see them all a day or two later in freedom. / Please get the watch & bring for the holiday.

All in all, my dear, I am v. close to you & your letter is a great excitement when it comes. It's all v. dream like – as freedom often is to me. But here indeed it's stronger. I, actually in prison, seems something so natural & yet so little like a dream existence. It's enhanced, you see, by not feeling or being a criminal. I got terribly excited on Sat, the 8th, thinking of the music outside. And there are whole days of impatience – days also of boredom. Wonderful moments like the hundreds of men's voices singing the old hundredth – & that brings tears. One is rather emotional, naturally. & frightfully self-conscious. We all are. That takes a bit of time to go afterwards I believe. Quaker meeting means a lot. One is also closer to the spirit in here, by the act of cutting off. I've never felt it more strongly, tho I can't as yet go the violent ascetic way & but I have a sense of cleaning the grooves by means of it. The spirit shines clearer than one – it may affect the music I think, gradually. And I think the Symphony was gain by this enforced rest. I'm pretty certain of it itself, anyhow & I think I shall pull it off. But I've decided to set the 4 let movement done first. Give my love to all v at the — but then on. Michael v I am not here etc.

In replying to this letter, please write on the envelope:—

16.8.43

Number ...5832... **Name** .... M.K. Tippett ....

.... WORMWOOD SCRUBS .... Prison

The following regulations as to communications, by Visit or Letter, between prisoners and their friends are notified for the information of their correspondents.

The permission to write and receive letters is given to prisoners for the purpose of enabling them to keep up a connection with their respectable friends.

All letters are read by the Prison Authorities. They must be legibly written and not crossed. Any which are of an objectionable tendency, either to or from prisoners, will be suppressed.

Prisoners are permitted to receive and to write a letter at intervals, which depend on the rules of the stage they attain by industry and good conduct; but matters of special importance to a prisoner may be communicated at any time by letter (prepaid) to the Governor, who will inform the prisoner thereof, if expedient.

In case of misconduct, the privilege of receiving and writing a letter may be forfeited for a time.

Money, Postage Stamps, Food, Tobacco, Clothes, etc., should not be sent to prisoners for their use in Prison, as nothing is allowed to be received at the Prison for that purpose.

Persons attempting to communicate with prisoners contrary to the rules, or to introduce any article to or for prisoners, are liable to fine or imprisonment, and any prisoner concerned in such practices is liable to be severely punished.

Prisoners' friends are sometimes applied to by unauthorised persons, to give or send money, under pretence that it will be for the benefit of the prisoners. The people who make these requests are trying to get money for themselves by fraudulent pretences. If the friends of a prisoner are asked for money, either verbally or by letter, they should at once inform the Governor of the Prison about the matter, and send him any letter they have received.

Prisoners are allowed to receive visits from their friends, according to rules, at intervals which depend on their stage.

When visits are due to prisoners, notification will be sent to the friends whom they desire to visit them.

No. 243 (15717—19 4-23)

Sun. Evelyn dearest - at last the final letter - a few days to go - Am ever so sorry to hear of yr pneumonia & hope indeed it is as slight as you suggest & that it has in its wake of a rest & that you're back now at home. John on visit last Thursday told me you were still in hospital then! Shall be so delighted if you're at the gate on Sat, but I don't know how sensible an early rise will be for you - ? if you can't come will you let Britten know - if you still feel I ought to be met by some one - failing B.B. John will be preferable. For you to get here you go from Chiswick by train or bus to Hammersmith or Shepherd's Bush & get a bus north going Wilby buses, who go from Reform to the latter & on to Wood Lane Und. Stn after 'White City' the next stop or so is Du Cane Avenue - you ask for that - straight along the road abt ¼ of a mile. I believe its 7.30 to 7.45 or so, release - but will wait for you. If Ben B. is to come his quickest way other than cross-going taxi - is Tube via Oxford Circus to Wood Lane, Trolley bus to Du Cane - (2 stops?).

Hope John gave you message to add my leatherbelt to the clothes list - tho watch. Now about my final & proper home coming. I'm so impatient for the cottage & work that I am not staying away longer than I planned, but will definitely travel up from Taunton (& David) on Thurs= Sept 24th. & try & get the 2.30 down from Victoria. Perhaps you cld meet at the 'Harbr' - 3.35 or so - & come over to tea. And bring some marzarine if you can, as I may not have much rations after sharing with Schwan Brothr & David's mother - & the week-end to go. And ask Miriam if she cld keep me some eggs for the week end for suppers & then we can start normally the following week. Give my love to Miriam & say I'm dying to be home, & that even Cornwall is only necessity & poor sense. And let us all pray that I shall be left in peace now because I'm so full of music. Also, Felix Aprahamian who came with John & Aprahamian on visit wanted to pencil the L.P.O. for the first perf. of the Symphony, subject to publisher's approval - & for the spring! Well. they will have to wait. Yet it's great fun to have offers thro' the glass window of visitor's box! & shows how the pathetic & performances are beginning to tell.

John told me tho Durke chair, who will earn 20 guns from B.B.C. for the

Siebs recording, want me to have to balance after singers' expenses etc, for my holiday. Isn't that a nice gesture? So we can all have a good time. Excessions across the Bar by firms to such cheerful holidayish items.

I've written mother about Rose - just to tell her that of course I'll go to Tunbridge whichever way it goes, but that in fact it will prevent any real family intimacy, put me on edge - & after 9 weeks imprisonment, quite the worst thing for Rose, or me. She had better face up to the fact that she will just spoil my (& her) homecoming - for the old usual mother-ish moral reasons which spoilt so much of childhood. I had a fearsome, but illuminating, dream on that a night past. It must have been quite the most decisive emotional influence of my upbringing. It's as well to attempt to assimilate it now that the possibility has arrived at looking at it dispassionately, as far as the personalities are concerned.

I don't think I've quite reached the point of being ready for memories & their refreshment - except occasionally - but I anticipate it. As yet, it's still plans & the future - only not in so youthful a manner as earlier. The music particularly is fairly concrete & serious - tho apparently much more ahead to be done than already created. There won't be able for a year or more - & a fair number of good launchings - like the oratorio. Bergmann told me (the way that he's nearly completed the first reading of the proofs. So that goes forward & will be out in the autumn - a good time. Meanwhile I hope to get Steffens to print the "Boyhoods End" - which had good reviews & unexpected ones. Sept 4th. at Morley is a Bergmann concert - choir is not till Oct 16th. (Weelkes.) Tho' that means a lot of work already. Dr Bultach rather jockeyed me (or I did myself) into giving Wed. evenings to a Morley orchestra - but since then I've given a message to John at visit to try & keep it at bay - at least for the beginning of term. I just must write & everything else must & will have to wait. The November concert B.B. refers to is a proper Britten-Tippett do, ½ financed by L.P.O. Col. Clifford

Curzon to play my Sonata, +2.pf: work of Britten's with him –
P.P. to sing Michaelangelo's 'Boyhood's End' – props also
something else of Britten's. A nice show? I gather that Holmes
is toying with letting Suchi repeat the Double Concerto at a Boosey's
Hawkes concert – I do hope it comes off. Sellick is down to play the
Sonata at Nat. Gallery in Sept 21 or 22: probably which. So things are
not too bad – & John decided to begin negotiations with Bliss to
redeem his promise to do the Fantasia broadcast after the prom.
season.

Yes props its tête à tête breakfast with Pete & Ben à trois. And
lunch? It looks like a crowd, o not really a crowd. I fancy
if you can but make the early morning that's nice & then tea
our Thurs: Sept 2nd in our proper surroundings. Oh, that will
be a good day.

As I feel now, I'd go to mother's on Sunday 29th – move to
David's at Taunton on Tuesday afternoon 31st – leave the same
on the Thursday morning – two nights at each of them – & the Wed:
David can plan an expedition. He will think I ought to take more
holiday as I can, but he can't have it. I know that after 10 days
of holiday & differing company, decent clean food & fresh air,
I shall be champing to get back & let out the dammed-up
stream of sound. First the fanfare for Brass – then the 4th movement –
then a short break & re-visit Exmouth probably. Hofentlich all this
by mid-October – other the real thing – the new symphony, wh is
very much getting up steam.

As this letter tells you, I'm already living outside the
prison – I try not to get in a fever. But occasionally I do; the
not for long or seriously. By the time this gets you. if it
does in time the thing will be virtually over – & I have little
wish to repeat it – but of course will do so if driven.

Have made some very good friends & seen a great slice of life
so to speak. Extraordinarily childlike if not frankly childish. But
all of a piece with the army, factory life & all other mass phenomena.
We are indeed "such stuff as dreams are made of" – I become more
drawn to Shakespeare this viewpoint – only in another age's setting. Love
to you, my dear, & mops withee you Sat. Michael

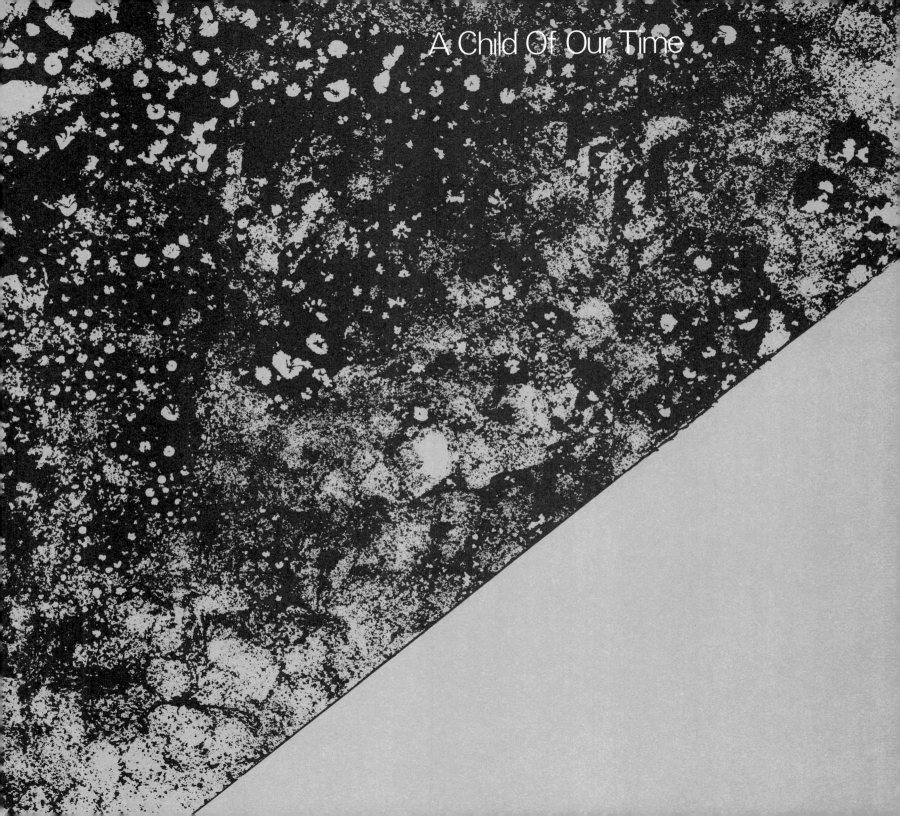

A Child Of Our Time

I hold for myself that the composition of oratorio and opera is a collective as well as a personal experience. While indeed all artistic creation may be seen in that way, I believe the collective experience, whether conscious or unconscious, is more fundamental to an oratorio or an opera than to a string quartet. If the traditional forms of oratorio or opera can contain the collective experiences of any time then composers generally will use them. I am driven to believe that traditional forms of oratorio like the Biblical Passions do not now always do this, even where individual persons and composers may hold the contrary. I find that there are unresolved but deeply serious collective experiences of our time which will not get themselves successfully into the traditional modes of expression.

I first became aware of this, as it concerned my activity as a composer, when the oratorio *A Child of Our Time* began the long process of gestation. In that example the collective experience was partly conscious (the experience of rejection, whether as individual, class or race) and partly unconscious (the experience of involvement in some uncontrollable catastrophe). I was able to use traditional Lutheran and Handelian Passions and oratorios as a technical basis, even down to the use of Negro spirituals in the place of the Lutheran Chorales. But the modern experience keeps bursting out of the older forms. I took a half-line from Eliot's *Murder in the Cathedral* as motto:

. . . the darkness declares the glory of light.

In this half-line the traditional Biblical words have been changed in order that they may reflect modern sensibilities. *A Child of Our Time* constantly plays the same trick. Not only in the words, which I wrote myself, but in the music too. It is even apparent in the spirituals, which do not derive from Eliot or myself.

Verbally the text reached an affirmation at the end before the final spiritual. The solo tenor sings: 'I would know my shadow and my light, so shall I at last be whole.' This contrast of division and wholeness has appeared already in this book* before *Moving Into Aquarius* in the 1944 essay: 'Contracting Into Abundance'. I used there the words: 'The only concept we can place over gainst the fact of divided man is the idea of the whole man.' And I immediately followed those words with an example taken from the history of opera, saying that the most enchanting expression of a general state where theological man is balanced against natural man is Mozart's *Magic Flute*. So it is clear to me that already as the first performances of *A Child of Our Time* were being given, I was toying with the idea of trying to give dramatic expression to the experiences of knowing the shadow and the light, and of wholeness, not by the method of example and contemplation proper to an oratorio, but by the method of action and consequence proper to an opera.

© Michael Tippett: excerpt from *Moving Into Aquarius* published by Paladin Books and reproduced by kind permission of Routledge and Kegan Paul Ltd.

The Accused Await Their Trial
Abraham Grynsban and his wife, uncle and aunt of the boy who shot Vom Rath, gave him shelter after an expulsion order had been made against him. They were sentenced to imprisonment by a Paris court for doing so.

The
GRYNSBAN CASE

The world awaits the trial of Herschel Grynsban, whose shooting of a German diplomat launched the Nazi pogrom. Preliminary move has been sentencing of Grynsban's uncle and aunt.

The Man Who Will Defend Grynsban
Maître Moro Giafferi defended the aunt and uncle; he is one of three famous lawyers who will defend Herschel Grynsban. A Corsican, he is perhaps the most eloquent advocate in France.

WHEN Herschel Grynsban shot Vom Rath in Paris nearly three months ago, it became certain at once that his trial would be of international importance. Justifying their savage pogrom after the shooting, the Nazis declared Grynsban was the agent of a Jewish world conspiracy ; their enemies, that—like Van der Lubbe, the Dutch youth who was beheaded for firing the Reichstag—he was the dupe of Nazi *agents provocateurs*. Germany, and her friends in France, brought pressure to have him tried quickly and secretly; democrats all over the world urged a public trial.

In the United States, Dorothy Thompson, journalist wife of Sinclair Lewis, formed a committee, collected funds, and briefed three famous French lawyers, Moro Giafferi, Henri Thorès and Weil Goudchaux, to defend Grynsban.

Preliminary judicial moves have been trial of Grynsban's uncle and aunt, German refugees, who sheltered him in Paris after an expulsion order had been made against him. They did not know where he could go. He had no passport—the world was closed to him. So they hid him in their home, were arrested after the shooting, but found innocent of complicity. For sheltering their nephew, they were sentenced to four months' prison and a small fine. On appeal, the uncle's sentence was increased to six months, the aunt's reduced to three. And Herschel Grynsban? He sits in Fresnes prison, reads, fasts on Thursdays to atone, declares he acted on his own. Waits, with the world, for his trial.

Grynsban's Aunt Breaks Down As She Hears The Story Told
While hiding with his uncle and aunt, Herschel Grynsban got a letter from his parents.
It told him of their sufferings under the Nazi persecution in Germany. This letter led him
to shoot Vom Rath. As Giafferi reads the letter in Court, Grynsban's aunt breaks down.

Where Herschel Grynsban Is Imprisoned
The prison of Fresnes. Behind these walls, the 17-year-old boy for whose mad act
hundreds of thousands of Jews have been savagely punished, still awaits trial. Mean-
time his aunt and uncle were tried for having sheltered him.

Men Without a Country
Himself a refugee, Abraham Grynsban tells the Court
that he felt it his duty to shelter his nephew until he
could find a country where the boy would be safe.

A CHILD OF OUR TIME

An Oratorio by

MICHAEL TIPPETT

═══════════════════════════════

The first performance of this work will be given at the ROYAL ADELPHI THEATRE, *on Sunday, March 19th, at 2.30, by* JOAN CROSS, MARGARET McARTHUR, PETER PEARS, NORMAN WALKER, LONDON REGION CIVIL DEFENCE & MORLEY COLLEGE CHOIRS, *and the* LONDON PHILHARMONIC ORCHESTRA *conducted by* WALTER GOEHR. *(It will be preceded by the Mauerische Trauermusik (K477) and the Symphony in G minor (K183) of* MOZART*).*

═══════════════════════════════

AN ACCOUNT OF THE ORATORIO IS GIVEN OVERLEAF

═══════════════════════════════

Tickets may be obtained from the Box Office (Temple Bar 7611)

(1d.

ARNE AND FAURE AT ALBERT HALL

DISLIKE OF EMPHASIS

Edric Cundell, who conducted the Philharmonic concert in the Albert Hall on Saturday, gave us two compositions whose authors seemed to share a natural distaste for emphasis and over-statement—Arne and Fauré.

The Englishman's overture in B flat has most of the features which have kept Arne's name alive. Fauré's suite, "Pelléas and Melisande," on the other hand, lacks some of the finer touches of his best work.

Beethoven's fourth piano concerto, admirably played by Solomon, and Schubert's C major symphony completed the unusual but interesting scheme.

Aiding Dr. Barnardo's

A concert in aid of Dr. Barnardo's Homes was attended by a large audience at the Kingsway Hall on Saturday. An orchestra recently formed by its conductor, Frederick Bailey, gave a spirited reading of familiar music. — F. B.

A Worldly Oratorio

"A Child of Our Time," a secular oratorio of which text and music are by Michael Tippett, was given its first performance at the Adelphi Theatre yesterday afternoon.

Its subject is the shooting of a German diplomat in Paris by a Jewish lad which is made the pretext for an aggravated pogrom. The words are of effective simplicity, and the music has a highly individual quality that reveals great skill.

The performance was due to the initiative of the London Philharmonic Orchestra and was conducted by Mr. Walter Goehr.

Oratorio with modern theme

THE choral work for which we have been waiting since the outbreak of this war, written by a British composer on a contemporary theme and in a contemporary idiom, has at length appeared.

Michael Tippett's "A Child of Our Time," heard for the first time at the London Philharmonic Orchestra's concert at the Adelphi yesterday, is a work which immediately fires the imagination, and is, I think, in its strange, very individual way completely successful; or at least it will be when the performance is tightened up.

The tale behind it is an actual occurrence in Paris in 1938, the shooting of a German diplomat by a Jewish boy, who is then tried and eventually "disappears."

The music is very able, intensely moving and remarkably varied in texture and emphasis.

The performers were the London Region Civil Defence and Morley College Choirs, with Joan Cross, Margaret McArthur, Peter Pears and Roderick Lloyd as soloists. Walter Goehr conducted.

One is bound to congratulate these players and singers, who did such competent work in unpropitious circumstances.

S. Maude   **Scott Goddard**

there should be advisory committees in each area so that local needs are met.

" A CHILD OF OUR TIME "

TIPPETT'S NEW ORATORIO

The London Philharmonic Orchestra yesterday devoted its Sunday afternoon concert at the Adelphi Theatre to the production of a new oratorio, *A Child of Our Time*, by Michael Tippett.

The choral work was prefaced by an interesting excursion into unfamiliar Mozart—namely, the Maurerische Trauermusik and a remarkable early symphony in G minor scored with four horns. Mr. Walter Goehr conducted and gave a convincing account of the whole programme of unusual music.

As a rule music requires even more of the process called " distancing " by psychologists and " recollection in tranquillity " by Wordsworth than do the other arts of painting, drama, and literature in assimilating contemporary events into their artistic substance. Tracts for the times are not easy to write in music, though Vaughan Williams produced one in *Dona nobis pacem*; indeed, tracts are not easy to write in music at all, though Parry spent the last part of his life in attempting it. Tippett has succeeded to a quite remarkable extent in creating a powerful work out of a contemplation of the evil abroad in the world of yesterday and to-day. Perhaps because he has written his own text in terse, pregnant sentences he has succeeded in combining the force of the particular with the significance of the universal. He writes a spare and tense counterpoint, not unlike Holst's, and then eases the tension alike in the philosophy and the music by introducing a negro spiritual for all the world as though it were a chorale of Bach's. Not the slightest incongruity is felt, since the spiritual expresses a universal idea and a universal emotion in the simplest terms.

The names of Parry, Bach, and Holst suggest that the new work is in the tradition of oratorio. It is. But it is strikingly original alike in conception and execution. A proof of the originality of the actual music is the new virtue which the composer finds in a common chord in root position. The work is not easy to sing, but choir (Civil Defence and Morley College) and soloists (Misses Joan Cross and Margaret McArthur, Messrs. Peter Pears and Roderick Lloyd) grasped its purport with sure understanding, and the audience listened intently.   S. Maude

NATIONAL GALLERY CONCERTS

The National Gallery programmes are as follows:—

To-day.—Piano recital by Mr. Colin Horsley.
To-morrow.—Programme of Wolf's lieder sung by Miss Winifred Radford and Mr. Norman Walker.
Wednesday.—The Grinke Ensemble and Miss Denise Lassimonne will play a Beethoven programme.
Thursday.—Recital by the Fleet Street Choir.
Friday.—Violin sonatas played by Miss Kersey and Miss Long.

In the Corn Exchange, Bedford, Michael Tippett, a Lonely Figure, Listens to a Rehearsal of His Work
To his left, the four soloists, Joan Cross, Margaret McArthur, Peter Pears, and Roderick Lloyd, standing among the choir, are singing the Spiritual "Steal Away to Jesus," which the composer has woven into the Oratorio. Performing with them is the B.B.C. Symphony Orchestra, conducted by Walter Goehr.

A COMPOSER LISTENS TO HIS OWN ORATORIO

Michael Tippett's Oratorio, a "Child of Our Time"—one of the most interesting achievements in music produced for many years in Britain—is being performed at the Albert Hall on Wednesday, February 28, by the London Philharmonic Orchestra and two choirs, in aid of the children of Warsaw.

Photographed by H. MAGEE

THE oratorio is to music what the Miracle Play was to drama—a representation of the conflict in man's soul, and of his redemption through faith. With its simple opposition of good and evil, the Miracle Play died, giving way to a more sophisticated drama in which modern man, sceptical and materialistic, looked for other answers to his problems than religion. By the twentieth century, the Passion of Christ, which had tormented the conscience of Europe for nearly 2,000 years, no longer inspired oratorios like those of Handel, Bach and Mendelssohn; the suffering of the hungry, the tortured, and the dying, had become commonplace— the theme of living rather than of art, a stimulus to revolt rather than to music. Both artists and people seemed to have become blind to the world's Passion, because it was all around them. And the oratorio, with its voices crying out against the chorus of the mob, with its soprano of pity and its tenor of defiance, answering the bass of tyranny and evil, seemed as dead as the Miracle Play.

Michael Tippett, raising the form from its recent neglect, has written an oratorio of our times. He has discarded the "sacred" conventions of his predecessors, but his secular theme has the deepest spiritual purpose of religious music.

"I don't remember precisely how a *Child of Our Time* first came into my head," he says. "I can remember being much affected by Grynspan's shooting of von Rath at the German Legation in

The Score of a "Child of Our Time"
This is the original score, since published for the use of Choral Societies by Schott & Co., Ltd.

Paris in the autumn of '38. And I remember listening, on Christmas Day of that year, to the broadcast of Berlioz's lovely *Childhood of Christ*, and afterwards trying to think out what had become nowadays of the emotional power in the once universally accepted image of the Christ Child, a power which at one time could make all Europe bend its knee—at least for a season. The real beginning of a *Child of Our Time* was the moment when Grynspan's act and Jesus, who *voluntarily* died for sins, became the strands which formed, as it were, a new-old pattern. And this pattern seemed to me expressible only in an oratorio—which is, by convention, a religio-dramatic musical form. Bit by bit, the drama sorted itself out into chorus, scena, airs and recitative. But there was still something missing which was traditional for the Lutheran Passions—and that was the chorales, which the composer chose from the great hymnals of the time, according to his needs as to words and music. The effect of the chorales was something like a popular commentary on the divine story.

"Now, I didn't imagine that any such general melodies existed in our time, until, by chance, one Sunday I listened-in to a man singing negro songs. I remember he sang them very badly, but when he came to a phrase in the spiritual 'Steal Away,' I was shot through with the sudden realisation that the melody was far greater than the individual singer, and had the power to move us all. So I got hold of

Continued overleaf

Tippett Beats Time With His Finger
The thirty-nine-year-old composer listens in rapture to his work, murmurs "Heavenly music, heavenly music!"

THE FIRST VIOLINS
Paul Beard, leader of the B.B.C. Symphony Orchestra, concentrates on a difficult phrase in a muted passage.

THE CONDUCTOR
Walter Goehr, himself a composer, introduced the Oratorio to the general public.

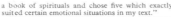

a book of spirituals and chose five which exactly suited certain emotional situations in my text."

Tippett finished the oratorio in 1941, and it was first performed at the Adelphi Theatre, London, on March 19, 1944, by the London Region Civil Defence and Morley College Choirs, and the London Philharmonic Orchestra, conducted by Walter Goehr. At once, it made an impression, as a fervently sincere, as well as a subtle, work of art. The older musical critics were doubtful.

"A political oratorio, humph!" they said, listening with half an ear while the other half mentally enjoyed a few phrases from the Siegfried Idyll and the *Damnation of Faust*. "Good politics can make bad music. Let's congratulate Tippett on his intentions. And as for his spirituals, we'll say that the best parts of Tippett's oratorio are the spirituals. After all, he didn't write them." The younger critics had no doubts of the distinction which lay in a *Child of Our Time*. As a technician, Tippett's skill in the use of polyrhythm, the assurance of his counterpoint, and above all, the aptness of his orchestration,

THE DOUBLE BASSES
They express, at times, the forces of violence and oppression, in contrast to the tender themes of the violins.

THE BASS
Roderick Lloyd sings "Tell Old Pharaoh to Let the People Go."

THE SOPRANO
Joan Cross sings "Oh bye and bye I am going to lay down my heavy load."

20

indicated his unusual merits. As a composer, he found his justification in the powerful effect of his work on all who heard it.

To see Tippett at a rehearsal, is to repeat with him some of the birth-pangs of his oratorios. He twists in his chair, clutches his head with his hands, then walks around the empty hall with his eyes shut. His whole body becomes tense, as the voices of the choir swell out. In the middle of a passage for muted violins, Tippett hears a wrong note. He jumps like a man who has been insulted, and hurries to the conductor's dais. The orchestra pauses; the composer talks urgently, anxiously to Walter Goehr. A moment of explanation; the violinist's score has been wrongly transcribed. Tippett walks back to his chair, sinks into it, shuts his eyes; and the orchestra and voices begin again. "I have heard my oratorio often," says Tippett, "but I never fail to be moved by it." That isn't the boast of a vain man; it is an experience which many have shared.

What is there in a *Child of Our Time* which receives such an instant and vibrating answer in the feelings of the ordinary man and woman? Perhaps, it is that Tippett's oratorio with its pain, its ecstasy and its theme—"The simple-hearted shall exult in the end"—speaks the inexpressible thoughts of us all, children of our time, brothers and sisters in the modern agony.

MAURICE EDELMAN.

THE B.B.C. CHORUS SINGS

"Here is no final grieving, but an abiding hope. The moving waters renew the earth: it is spring." They echo the words, sung before by the four soloists.

64

MUSIC

By Scott Goddard *Smalle* 1945

Today's New Symphony

WHEN Michael Tippett's new Symphony is played for the first time in Liverpool this afternoon a work both significant and important will have been added to our contemporary music and we who have listened will have had a worth-while experience.

Of that I am certain, without having heard the music or even seen it at the moment of writing.

For nothing he has written during the last ten years has made me alter my opinion that Tippett (just 40 years of age) is a serious artist, one of the most able musicians of the younger set in this country and probably the most poetic nature of them all.

Having heard a man's music we turn for confirmation of things we have found in it to the man himself, hoping to discover some hint of what his spirit is. This is especially the case with contemporary composers whose music is not immediately clear.

MICHAEL TIPPETT - " *A serious artist* "

Perhaps something may be caught from looking at the musician; an instance is the memory of that fire in Bartok's eyes.

Tippett's profile is dominated by a fine head with its shock of black hair, a lean face and then the tall, spare frame. The lineaments are those of an already experienced being blessed, now, with a sense of humour.

It is only the lines on the face, some of them unusually deep for a man of his youth and youthful bearing, that recall his having paid richly during the war for his opinions. Otherwise, no sign of that nor any mention of it; although if you asked for information about tribunals and prisons, plenty would be given in Tippett's candid manner, as from one interested person to another.

For these happenings touched him closely and are at least one part of something fundamental in his philosophy. He has nothing to hide, is a voluble talker and if persuaded will talk about this too.

Hearing him talk one says: this is a voluble writer, surely? Yet he has let very little reach us. He is his own stern critic, and the final state of his music is a very concentrated version of his naturally exuberant thought. We shall hear this afternoon the latest point his thought has reached.

The Midsummer Marriage

There is up-to-date drama to be made out of the innumerable conflicts engendered by our ignorance or illusion about ourselves. So *The Midsummer Marriage* may not be singular in that only in the course of the plot do the characters become aware of their real selves. A classic instance, to my mind, is *The Family Reunion*, where Eliot conceives his hero as returning to the family precisely to discover the nature of the guilt he feels at having actually or psychologically (it seems to matter little that we never quite know which) pushed his wife overboard. In Act I he fails; and the Eumenides, when they appear, baffle him. In Act II he partially succeeds: and the Eumenides are tolerable.

Auden's *The Ascent of F6*, Eliot's *The Cocktail Party*, Fry's *A Sleep of Prisoners* (and many other plays) all use this technique. But more to my purpose is Shaw's *Getting Married*, because the hindrances to the eventual marriage of that comedy are caused, if I remember right, by the prospective couple re-examining, on the wedding morning, themselves and their intentions in the light of some book of Shavian moral doctrine. And it was with a blurred image of this situation in my mind's eye that I had my first illumination — that is, I *saw* a stage picture (as opposed to hearing a musical sound) of a wooded hilltop with a temple, where a warm and soft young man was being rebuffed by a cold and hard young woman (to my mind a very common present situation) to such a degree that the collective, magical archetypes take charge — Jung's *anima* and *animus* — the girl, inflated by the latter, rises through the stage flies to heaven, and the man, overwhelmed by the former, descends through the stage floor to hell. But it was clear they would soon return. For I saw the girl later descending in a costume reminiscent of the goddess Athena (who was born without father from Zeus's head) and the man ascending in one reminiscent of the god Dionysus (who, son of earth-born Semele, had a second birth from Zeus's thigh).

Even as I write now some of the excitement of these first pictures comes back. It is the feeling a creative artist has when he knows he has become the instrument of some collective imaginative experience — or, as Wagner put it, that a Myth is coming once more to life. I know that, for me, so soon as this thing starts, I am held willy-nilly and cannot turn back. But I know also that somewhere or other, in books, in pictures, in dreams, in real situations, everything is sooner or later to be found which *belongs* for all the details of the work, which is, as it were, ordained. And everything is accepted or rejected eventually according to whether it *fits* this preordained *thing*, which itself will not be fully known until it is finished.

Can Tippett do it?

5 March

OPERAS are the very devil. There must be something infernally fascinating about the operatic stage that lures composers to go through months and often years of grinding toil, knowing full well that their music is not the whole business and that they may be let down by a finely written but operatically valueless libretto, or by a faulty production.

Yet they go on hoping. And we, the public, fickle and in-

Scott Goddard

constant, judge the labour of years by one performance.

I am reminded of these matters by the announcement of a forthcoming event in the Festival Hall, one of the regular concerts of the Royal Philharmonic Society.

This will be conducted by the Master of the Queen's Music, Sir Arthur Bliss. All the music will be by him and included in the programme is the second act of his opera " The Olympians " in a concert version, of course.

Now " The Olympians " was first heard at Covent Garden in 1949, and it had none of the success that we had been led to expect.

Everything seemed set fair. An intriguing story by J. B. Priestley, an expert man of the stage, Peter Brook, to produce the work, all the resources of a great opera house and a fine orchestra.

But things went badly, and to this day " The Olympians " has not caught on.

Yet as far as Bliss's music is concerned there are exquisite things there, especially the opening of the second act, some of the most ravishing music Bliss has ever written.

This concert is on January 26.

The very next night another opera takes the stage at Covent Garden and again years of work will be judged by the audience at the first night of "The Midsummer Marriage," by Michael Tippett.

How will it go?

No one can tell. And will that first-night judgment be fair? First-night nerves play odd tricks and not only on the stage or in the orchestra pit but among the audience.

Tippett, writing his own libretto, presents a story of young love, a comedy spiced with bewilderments and frustrations

This opera makes great demands on singers, players and dancers, too, for there is an intricate ballet.

All in all, this will be one of the most exciting and incalculable first-nights in the whole history of British opera.

THIS OPERA BAFFLES US TOO, SAY SINGERS

TREE TAKES A BOW...

It's his idea

Bewilderment at Covent Garden

By JAMES THOMAS

NOT since Salvador Dali tried to introduce a flying hippopotamus into the cast of Strauss's "Salome" has the Royal Opera House had such a baffled cast on its hands as the one which will launch Michael Tippett's "The Midsummer Marriage" into the world tomorrow night.

It is the first opera in (more or less) modern dress which Covent Garden has staged. Its villain is a business tycoon called King Fisher, and it has a flight of stairs which leads up to heaven, with another which leads down to hell.

And the cast, after weeks of rehearsal, are still wondering just what it's all about.

The prima donna, Australia's Joan Sutherland, said yesterday: "Mr. Tippett told me not to worry if I didn't understand it. He said just to sing it as well as I could, and to leave the audience to work out the significance for themselves."

Not a timber yard

The Covent Garden official who showed me around at rehearsal yesterday tried desperately to give me an idea of the story, but finally admitted total failure.

On the stage the action appeared to be taking place in a timber yard encircled by a bright blue cyclorama.

I asked: "What are all those planks standing up on the left?"

"A wood," said the Covent Garden official miserably.

"And what do those dancers represent?"

"Trees, I think—dancing trees," said the C.G.O., plucking at his collar forlornly.

We met Otakar Kraus, the big businessman villain in a short black jacket and a blue waistcoat.

"If you are coming to ask me what it is all about, don't bother," said Mr. Kraus. "I don't know. I just cannot get over being asked to sing in my own spectacles—but I miss the usual operatic costumes to swish round."

You guess

Then Mr. Kraus looked disappointed. He added: "I thought that just for once I would be able to live an opera out. I always die. I die again in this. I drop dead through some sort of supernatural power. How? Your guess is as good as mine when it comes to this opera."

We met Edith Coates, in a bristly grey wig, three inch platform soles, and a navy blue coat. "What a get-up," said the C.G.O., with awe.

"What an opera," said Miss Coates. "I don't know who I am, and that's the truth. I am described as an Ancient. Let's be content with that."

We met John Lanigan, who supplies romantic interest as a mechanic. His comment: "I can only say that I know my part."

We met Senora Oralia Dominguez, imported regardless of expense from La Scala, Milan, to sing the part of a clairvoyante. Her eyes gazed mournfully out of a face painted bright blue.

In Italian she said: "The music is most interesting, but it is useless to talk to me of anything else. I am not even sure why my face is painted blue."

A kind of ...

Then we met Miss Barbara Hepworth, the sculptress and painter, who has designed the scenery and costumes. She was tripping round the back of the Grand Tier peering from different angles at a set which is described thus in the libretto (price 5s.):

"When fully lighted the stage, as seen from the audience, presents a clearing in a wood, perhaps at the top of the hill, against the sky. At the back of the stage is an architectural group of buildings, a kind of sanctuary, whose centre appears to be an ancient Greek temple."

Miss Hepworth said: "I draw all the costumes as if they had been carved, to get a sculptural effect. The set itself is a mixture of my style in painting and sculpture. It is mobile, you see."

Miss Olivia Cranmer, head of the wardrobe, put it this way: "What we've had to do is to turn human beings into statues and statues into human beings."

Perfectly simple

Finally, we met Mr. Tippett. He is 50, but looks 30. This is his first opera, and he has written words as well as music. The job took five years.

He said:

"I have gathered that the singers don't see what I'm getting at, but the whole thing seems perfectly simple to me.

"This is a story of two sets of lovers, and their different approach towards marriage. It is a piece of depth and imagination, and it is like a crystal ball which you can turn endless ways. The opera means what it says—nothing more."

MICHAEL TIPPETT
"It means what it says"

ONE of these three dancers in the opera is a tree. You can't guess which? Why — the one holding a bough. The bough is that wooden frame, of course. **(Right)** Edith Coates watches prima donna Oralia Dominguez paint her face blue. Why? Well, it's all part of the opera. No, it's no good asking the lady — she doesn't know, either

Pictures: John Silverside

Royal Opera House

COVENT GARDEN

THE ROYAL OPERA HOUSE, COVENT GARDEN, LIMITED

GENERAL ADMINISTRATOR . DAVID L. WEBSTER

HOUSE MANAGER . NEVILLE COPPEL

presents

THE WORLD PREMIÈRE OF

The Midsummer Marriage

OPERA IN THREE ACTS

Words and Music by MICHAEL TIPPETT

Scenery and costumes by BARBARA HEPWORTH

Choreography by JOHN CRANKO

CONDUCTOR - JOHN PRITCHARD

PRODUCER - CHRISTOPHER WEST

THURSDAY, 27th JANUARY, 1955

First Night S Mande

OPERA MARRED BY OBSCURITY

"THE MIDSUMMER MARRIAGE"

By MARTIN COOPER

For all its strangeness, Michael Tippett's "The Midsummer Marriage" is not unique of its kind in the operatic repertory. The libretto by the composer is a drama of spiritual illumination —the initiation of two pairs of lovers into the mysteries of the Higher Thought.

The theme is thus the same as that of Mozart's "Magic Flute," with a vague Steiner or Jung philosophy replacing Free-masonry and an all-too-sensible businessman in the Queen of the Night's role.

In Mozart's opera we know that humanity, wisdom and virtue are the lovers' goal and we see, in sublime pantomime, how it is achieved.

In Tippett's libretto the goal is obscure and the means by which it is reached obscurer. Both are veiled in an extraordinary jumble of verbal images and stage mumbo jumbo, which includes a crystal-gazing medium and two transfigurations, one Greek and the other Hindu.

CONCISENESS LACKING

Tippett's music cannot, unfortunately, wholly redeem this hotch-potch. Although the score is complex in texture, the musical language is fundamentally simple and its effect on the ear often beautiful.

Much of the choral writing especially—and the chorus plays a very large part—is ingenious and refined, though it has not the dramatic conciseness needed in the opera house.

The chief musical weakness of the whole opera lies in the absence of strong characterisation. The worlds of Light and Darkness are not sufficiently differentiated, and the representatives of each are musically almost interchangeable. The monotony that results is only relieved by the extensive ballet.

The music for these highly esoteric dances is the best in the opera, but John Cranko's ingenious choreography only succeeds in underlining the rather pretentious symbolism of the underlying idea. Barbara Hepworth's stage sets recalled those fashionable in Berlin some 30 years ago, effective in an austere and angular manner though not very practicable.

UGLY COSTUMES

The costumes on the other hand were depressingly ugly. But this was a small matter compared with what seemed the waste of much extraordinarily vital and original music on an impossible libretto.

The performance of this difficult work was in many ways a triumph for Covent Garden. The orchestra under John Pritchard did full justice to Tippett's rhythmic volubility and the imaginative quality of his orchestration.

Joan Sutherland and Richard Lewis and Adele Leigh and John Lanigan were well cast as the lovers, and Oralia Dominguez and Otakar Kraus made the most of somewhat unrewarding parts.

The Arts

ROYAL OPERA HOUSE

"THE MIDSUMMER MARRIAGE"

Strephon	Pirmin Trecu
The Ancients	Michael Langdon / Edith Coates
Mark	Richard Lewis
Jenifer	Joan Sutherland
King Fisher	Otakar Kraus
Bella	Adele Leigh
Jack	John Lanigan
Girl Dancer	Julia Farron
Sosostris	Oralia Dominguez

Conductor: John Pritchard

The premise on which Michael Tippett has written and composed his opera is that music is capable of conducting dramatic action on two planes of reality. The premise has been proved sound in *The Magic Flute*, and *The Magic Flute* is the allegorical prototype of *The Midsummer Marriage.*

The correspondence is discernible in the two pairs of lovers, in the initiation into the way of the life of wisdom, and even in such a detail as Papageno's philoprogenitive aria in Bella's little song to Jack. The main theme however, though similar in its approach through symbolism to the deeper meaning of life, is different: it is double significance of sexual love at the levels of biological purpose and of spiritual commission.

The theme is magnificent. Tippett's belief that music can conduct the argument at the two levels is right: symbolism and allegory convey their own meanings in spite of the obscurity of any particular myth in which they find expression. But one must play fair with symbolism and not mix myths or confusion takes the place of obscurity. Tippett has overloaded his allegory. Not content with an English midsummer and its folklore, he evokes Dionysus and Artemis and caps the mixture with the Indian lotus flower. The force behind the conception of the opera has been too much for his control: it is throughout the reversal of the Greek maxim "nothing too much"; there is too much of everything. Of counterpoint in the music—in this it resembles Hindemith's *Mathis der Maler*; of dramatic paraphernalia in the action—the last act nearly founders with the weight of it; of orchestration—almost all the words of maximum significance are extinguished with trombones. Yet such is the imaginative sweep, such the driving force of his musical invention, that despite the unnecessary burdens he has placed upon it the opera held its audience, declared its extraordinary vitality and astonished with its originality.

It is strange to complain of excess of counterpoint, but the incessant grinding of it in its strong rhythmic progress—it is in the last resort madrigalian counterpoint magnified a thousandfold—frets the nerves, and some extensive surgery in the first and third acts will be necessary. The second act is occupied with the Dances of the Seasons, for which Mr. John Cranko had found better choreography than he had elsewhere for the temple attendants to dance. Barbara Hepworth's scenery will divide opinion clean down the middle according to the view taken whether symbolism or abstraction is the right setting for the action. What we have is a kind of Stonehenge reconditioned for the Festival of Britain. Her dresses on the other hand are likely to win universal approval. The chorus of Mark's and Jenifer's friends was too large and confronted Mr. Christopher West with an insoluble problem of disposing them upon and moving them about the stage.

The singers have hardly less difficulty than conductor and producer, but they tackled it firmly and triumphed by their confidence, especially Miss Joan Sutherland and Mr. Richard Lewis, who have to act and sing upon the double plane. The other pair have a simpler task—they have only to be mundane —which Miss Adele Leigh and Mr. John Lanigan nevertheless accomplished with vivacity and charm. The only set aria in the opera, the vaticinations of Sosostris, was impressively sung by Miss Oralia Dominguez. Mr. Otakar Kraus sustained the character of King Fisher, who very nearly becomes a symbol of the capitalist armament king, with his great experience of professional villainy. The two Ancients were suitably hieratic. But for difficulty it is doubtful if anyone had so much to tackle as the conductor: Mr. John Pritchard was firm in control of the splintering rhythms, giving the music its self-generating impetus and only failing to repress the dynamics, more particularly at the beginning because at that point he dared not do anything to check the way on the craft he had just launched.

NONSENSE
—but it's MUSIC
A night at the opera ends with a mystery

OPERA : The Midsummer Marriage.
THEATRE : Covent Garden.

By CECIL SMITH

WHAT on earth does Michael Tippett's new opera mean ? Perplexed Covent Garden first-nighters asked one another this question during the intervals last night. Most of them still asked it when the opera was over.

The action (if that is the right word) takes place on Midsummer's Day. The scene — somewhat like a diagram from a textbook in advanced geometry—contains a grilled entrance to a cave at the left, a temple portico in the middle, and a stairway leading nowhere at the right.

The She-Ancient

Jenifer and Mark are supposed to get married in the first act. But Jenifer arrives in a street dress instead of a bridal costume, and refuses to go through with the wedding.

She goes up the stairway and disappears. Mark goes into the cave and disappears.

An American business man (rude and dictatorial, of course) and his secretary appear. They hold an obscure conversation with the He-Ancient and the She-Ancient, who emerge from the temple.

Jenifer returns, and goes into the cave. Mark returns and climbs the stairs.

And that is only the first of three acts. Would you like to hear about the dances—later on —in which a hound pursues a hare, an otter a fish, and a hawk a crippled bird ? Would you like to listen in on the visionary remarks of Sosostris, an all-wise clairvoyante ?

No ? Well, then, do you care that Jenifer and Mark finally get married and that the Big Bad Business Man falls dead ?

Get it ?

If you still wonder what "The Midsummer Marriage" means, the final explanation of the He-Ancient and the She-Ancient will make it clear :—

*"From heavenly One the Two divide
And Three as Paraclete can make
Symbolic union · with the Four."*

Get it ?

I consider this libretto— Tippett wrote it as well as the music—one of the worst in the 350-year history of opera. And what a pity: for Tippett's music is often astoundingly beautiful, and the stage production is

ADELE LEIGH, OTAKAR KRAUS
Big Business Man and secretary in a scene from the opera.

worthy of a dramatic masterpiece.

Perhaps because we are used to seeing silly things done on the stage in the name of art, the whole affair looks less silly in the opera house than it really is.

Somehow you gather that Tippett wants Jenifer and Mark to find the basis for a perfect union—spiritual and physical— and that he thinks they have found it at the end of Act Three.

I salute . . .

I lift my hat to the splendid work of the chorus and orchestra. And to all the principals — especially Joan Sutherland, Adele Leigh, Richard Lewis, and Otakar Kraus—for their mastery of vocal parts in which the over-busy orchestra seldom gives helpful cues.

I salute John Pritchard for one of the finest achievements of his career as a conductor; Christopher West for a production that somehow looks rational; and the audience for applauding the superb music in spite of the story.

Above everyone else I salute the American business man for the sanest words of the evening. "Now is this nonsense at its noon."

A BRILLIANT FAILURE—

—is how ELIZABETH FRANK describes the ballet in " Midsummer Marriage ":

JOHN CRANKO'S ritual dances occupy almost an entire act of the opera comprising The Earth in Autumn; The Waters in Winter; The Air in Spring and, finally— Fire in Summer. Barbara Hepworth's costumes, which attempt a blend of simple stylised Greek classicism with abstract symbolism do little to help the dancers.

Julia Farron, and her quarry, Pirmin Trecu, representing in turn the hound in pursuit of the hare, the otter in pursuit of the fish and the hawk menacing the bird, are constantly hampered in their acrobatics by the corps de ballet, representing the elements, who spend a great deal of their time lying about on the floor.

SALUTE, TO A NEW OPERA

By Scott Goddard

MICHAEL TIPPETT'S new opera " The Midsummer Marriage," produced for the first time at Covent Garden last night, had precisely the effect that I expected.

It provided an immense amount of splendid music; in fact, it turned out to be a music-lover's opera. Also it flattered us by taking for granted that we were intelligent enough to think while we listened.

The plot was said to be complicated. Really it is clear though very unusual. But what else should one have expected of one of the most individual composers among us today? There is more originality in this work than in any new opera I have heard in the last 12 months.

Not easy to sing

The performance, conducted with much understanding by John Pritchard, was very creditable to all concerned. This is not easy music to sing or to play. But it must surely be very rewarding. It certainly is to listen to : a remarkable and memorable experience for the hearer and the onlooker.

Barbara Hepworth's sets are an immense pleasure to the eye, full of entrancing invention.

Of the singers Richard Lewis as the young man Mark proved himself again an interpretative artist of remarkable insight. Joan Sutherland, as Jenifer, his betrothed, was admirable in voice and deportment.

Adele Leigh was charming as Bella the secretary, and John Lanigan excellent as her boy friend Jack.

There is great choral music in this opera and that, too, was done with great spirit. This opera is a strange and haunting work. There was warm applause at the end, all of it well deserved.

Dramatic and sinister

Cranko has an eye for the dramatic and sinister. The lithe, grey figure of the hawk with her spiked silver helmet, borne aloft by the trees, fluttering and evil, to swoop on her prostrate victim, leaves an unforgettable and strangely disturbing picture in the mind.

The music is remarkable, too, for its dramatic disquiet, but the net result is a brilliant failure, intriguing, uncomfortable and strangely disappointing.

Welsh National
Opera

The Midsummer
Marriage

78

A vision of youth, love, life and joy

MUSIC
DAVID CAIRNS

SINCE its first performance 21 years ago — to an audience divided between shock at what seemed the libretto's wilful obscuirty and half-acknowledgment of an extraordinary richness of musical invention — Tippett's opera **The Midsummer Marriage** has been slowly growing from a cult object, the enthusiasm of a handful of believers, to a work of conscious mastery and central significance. It is as though there were a force in it that nothing can stop. Incomprehension, scepticism, ridicule, fear of its technical difficulties — it was bound to overcome them in the end. Tippett's vision of joy and renewal of life — improbable fruit of the mid-twentieth century—*had* to be communicated, and not only through the music — the complete recording did that five years ago — but on the stage. With the production by the Welsh National Opera which opened in Cardiff last week, this has now happened.

The event is crucial in two ways. It proves that an opera notorious for its problems—problems of technique and interpretation—is in fact well within a provincial company's resources, and secondly that in an unpretentious production which faces it straight on, the piece works. If this sounds lukewarm praise, the very opposite is intended. The point is the degree of dedication and intelligence with which those resources are used. The WNO performance is pre-eminent in both qualities. It is above all a triumph of teamwork; and the result is to make the opera, for the first time in the theatre, an integrated work of art, a coherent dramatic experience, in which music, text, declamation, solo and choral song, lighting, gesture, mime, dance are fused into a composite language of expressive power.

Played, sung, acted and danced like this (and experienced for the first time in a smallish theatre) "The Midsummer Marriage" throws off the awkwardness and confusions that seemed once to encumber its beauties; it becomes, with all its complexity of allusions and intertwining metaphors, a work of marvellous directness, fresh, unhampered, and young. I don't think that this overwhelming impression of youthfulness is simply the consequence of a predominantly youthful cast for whom the opera's imagery and terms of reference present no stumbling block but are on the contrary perfectly natural. But because they accept it, we accept it; and the conviction they put into it blazes out into the theatre and involves us with them in a communal celebration.

The ancient hilltop temple in the woodland clearing, inhabited by beings from a former age, the sub-hippy young men and women, the action shifting without warning between temporal and spiritual reality, the personifications of Jungian archetypes, the Shavian mechanic, secretary and big business man —how was it, one wonders, that we ever found this mixture misconceived, ill-digested, trendy? The difficulties have simply vanished.

I write in the present tense because Wednesday's performance remains so vivid. I can still hear the attack and conviction of the WNO orchestra in those exultant opening pages, and the sound of the superb chorus whose firm, incisive tone and exact chording showed at once that all would be well. It is no disrespect to the excellent cast to single out the chorus as the central character and the key to the whole achievement. This is the first time "The Midsummer Marriage" has been performed by a chorus that both looks and sounds young, and therefore the first time either that Mark's and Jenifer's friends could be shown as a credible group of people, forming an essential part of the drama, not an appendage, or that the full force and range of Tippett's choral writing in all its rhythmic vitality and splendour of sonority could be made evident.

Equally important is the way the element of dance is from the first integrated into the action. While retaining their otherness as acolytes of the temple, the dancers—silvery near-naked figures of Blake-like simplicity and sinewy grace—draw gradually closer to the human actors as the separate dimensions of spirit and flesh increasingly merge into one, until the sexual union they mime in the fourth and final Ritual Dance is simultaneously enacted at either side of the stage by the chorus. Terry Gilbert's choreography, whose style mixes the symbolic and the naturalistic in ideal proportion in the mime of Act 1 and the three Ritual Dances of Act 2, rises to this even greater challenge with what one would call perfect tact if the phrase didn't suggest an inhibitedness far removed from the passion and tenderness of the scene, an unequivocal representation of "carnal love through which the race of men is everlastingly renewed."

This scene is one of many unobtrusively right touches in Ian Watt Smith's staging, which only seems unambitiously plain until you realise how often he finds the grouping or gesture to serve music and drama (though he disappointingly shirks presenting Mark and Jenifer clearly at the climax of the vision in Act 3). Above all, he makes the action seem natural. Ralph Koltai's single set—enlivened by Annena Stubbs's simple but telling costumes and beautifully lit by Robert Ornbo (except that the pre-dawn scene in Act 3 is too bright)— presents a grassy amphitheatre, surmounted by the temple gates in the form of two large green superimposed wheels whose contrary revolutions open or close the gates—a serviceable framework, with a touch of the magical in it.

The soloists are worthy of chorus, orchestra and dancers. Helen Watts's Sosostris and Raimund Herincx's King Fisher are familiar figures (though Mr Herincx, more genial and relaxed than before, is consequently more formidable), but the rest are new. Mary Davies's Bella and Arthur Davies's Jack make a sweet-voiced pair of lovers, Paul Hudson and Maureen Guy are sonorous Ancients, John Treleaven an arden Mark, and Jill Gomez the embodiment of Tippett's rapt, exalted "child of the starry heaven," who only needs to project her words more clearly to be an ideal Jenifer. Richard Armstrong, who got to know the work as a repetiteur at Covent Garden, and whose belief in it led to the WNO's putting it on, conducts with fire, subtlety and complete conviction, animating and inspiring the whole enterprise, which indeed seems as though touched by some special miraculous grace. But really it is no more or less than the fruit of intelligence, love, and thorough preparation, applied to a masterpiece which from now on will need no more special pleading. The production can be seen in Cardiff on Thursday, and then in Birmingham, Liverpool, Leeds and Manchester, as part of the company's autumn tour.

King Priam

"KING PRIAM" REVEALS A MASTER OF OPERA

BRILLIANT, VITAL SCORE OF TIPPETT'S TROJAN DRAMA

From MARTIN COOPER

COVENTRY, Tuesday.

MICHAEL TIPPETT'S new opera, "King Priam," enjoyed a great and well-deserved success at its first performance by the Covent Garden Opera Company in the Coventry Theatre here this evening.

The great hopes aroused by his first opera, "The Midsummer Marriage," have been more than fulfilled, for both Tippett's libretto and music reveal a new certainty of aim and unity of purpose, as well as a new mastery of musical language.

"King Priam" is the tragedy of a man forced to choose between private affection and public duty and faced, whichever way he turns, by disaster that seems wholly unmerited.

His younger son Paris, the anti-hero of the work, is justified by his physical beauty, which wins him his counterpart Helen, while the elder son Hector and his wife Andromache represent honour and duty.

THREE GODDESSES
Jealous machinations

The three goddesses between whom Paris must choose are music-ally identified with his mother, his sister-in-law and his mistress, and Troy falls to the Greeks through their jealous machinations. Their instrument is Achilles, who represents the Greek temperament at its most brutal and capricious.

Tippett symbolises his characters by instrumental timbres and rhythms, and there are many scenes entirely dominated by a single instrumental line or group —solo cello, guitar, violins, piano and brass (the piano plays a very important part throughout) and harp and strings are all used in this way.

The result is a score of great and individual rhythmic vitality, filled with colour and light and mostly airy textures, which heighten the effect of those ensembles or choruses where vocal polyphony and instrumentation are deliberately more complex.

A three-man chorus explaining and commenting on the drama skil-fully connects the scenes and only occasionally, in the last act, unduly holds up the action.

EMPHASIS OF DESIGNS
Camp v city

In Sean Kenny's brilliantly coloured and severely stylised sets the distinction between the Trojan city and the Greek camp is effec-tively emphasised by abstract designs thrown on to the backcloth.

Sam Wanamaker's production is correspondingly powerful and economical and the collaboration of these two artists may well inaugurate a new chapter in British operatic production.

The standard of singing was uni-formly high, with Richard Lewis's Achilles notably outstanding. Margreta Elkins and John Dobson successfully suggested the plastic as well as the musical characters of Helen and Paris and Forbes Robinson brought great dignity and pathos to the title role, especially in the deeply moving scene where Priam learns of Hector's death.

Marie Collier's Hecuba, Jose-phine Veasey's Andromache and Victor Godfrey's Hector were all equally successfully characterised.

John Pritchard and the Covent Garden Orchestra were triumphantly successful in handling with easy virtuosity the many difficulties of this most original score.

AND IN COVENTRY LAST NIGHT . . .

Tippett strikes a blow for English opera

Michael Tippett's opera King Priam had its world premiere at the Coventry Theatre last night and in doing so struck a reverberating blow for the glory and genius of English opera.

Tippett has used the history of Troy from the birth of Paris to the death (which it causes) of his father Priam, and he has used it to create a timeless moral fable of destiny and choice in human affairs.

But there is none of the woolliness that Tippett's critics have liked to point out in the past. The opera is a brilliant piece of theatre whose tragic concepts are brought simply and superbly to life by the force of the music.

This music is not quite like anything he has written before. It is spare, taut, angular, often dissonant, sometimes hard to listen to, with none of the rich, teeming orchestral texture of his other opera, The Midsummer Marriage.

It is Tippett influenced by later Stravinsky, but it is Tippett through and through, and from the first thrilling fanfares to the last sight of compassion in the orchestra, with few exceptions it bears the action forward with power and sweep.

World stature

I fancy that after this opera (which comes to Covent Garden next Tuesday), we shall hear no more of Tippett the eccentric, the inspired amateur whose talent is not equal to his genius.

With King Priam he stands forth as a composer of unmistakable world stature.

The Covent Garden company, conducted by John Pritchard and produced by Sam Wanamaker, do it proud. Sean Kenny' designs are the most beautiful and inventive seen on our operatic stage for years. The excellent cast is led by Forbes Robinson's dignified and moving Priam.

Adam Bell

Reproduced by arrangement
with The Evening Standard.

Coventry Theatre

KING PRIAM

Reviewed by Andrew Porter

Hermes' aria, an interlude before the final scene, makes a good starting point for any consideration of Michael Tippett's second opera, *King Priam*, which had its première at the Coventry Festival last night. In the first act we see the birth of Paris, Priam's decisions, first to kill him, then to accept him into Troy, though this means his own death. And then Paris' reckless but inevitable choice of Aphrodite—and Helen.

Eloquent Mirror

Act Two is a lyrical slow movement, Achilles' song (with guitar accompaniment) within the sober glitter of a war scherzo. Now, in the third act, Hector has been killed; Priam has gone to Achilles' tent to redeem his son's body, and the two men—old king and dazzling hero, each fated to be killed by the other's son—are reconciled in the calm, tragic acceptance of personal and public catastrophe. Priam has become a visionary, an eloquent mirror of all men, who have been forced to choose between two evils and suffer the consequences of their choice. At this point Hermes comes forward to speak for the composer-librettist. Addressing the audience, he says:

Do not imagine all the secrets of life can be known from a story.
Oh, but feel the pity and the terror as Priam dies.
He already breathes an air as from another planet.
The world where he is going . . .
Cannot communicate itself through him,
But through the timeless music. . . .

O stream of sound,
In which the states of soul
Flow, surfacing and drowning,
While we sit watching from the bank
The mirrored world within. . . .

Or in plain, less hermetic prose: (1) *King Priam* is not a simple moral fable, but a tragedy. Tippett is not "saying" that Priam's choice was right or wrong, or that man's choice is, or is not, always overruled by destiny. He invites us to watch the consequences of a choice, to experience suffering and be wiser and more pitiful for it. And (2) the meaning of the opera lies not in the words alone; and in fact its last, hardest meaning, is something that its creator can communicate only by his music.

Aristotle's Definition

There are other things too, to be learnt from the passage. The allusion in the second line (" the pity and terror ") to Aristotle's famous definition of tragedy reminds us that Tippett chose the Trojan war as " an event having magnitude." He might have written about a para in Algeria having to choose between obedience and humanity when ordered to torture a prisoner; or about a King forced to choose between his throne and exile with the woman he loved; or about a president deciding whether any circumstances could justify the dropping of an atomic bomb. The last, certainly, would have had magnitude—but hardly the dramatic effectiveness or symbolic magnitude of the epic which has stirred the imagination of Europe for over 2,000 years.

The third line of the quotation is an adaptation from the Stefan George's poem in Schoenberg's Second String Quartet (and, in fact, Hermes' melody, probably not by coincidence, contains all the 12 notes of the chromatic scale). This reminds us that in a published essay Tippett linked the " air from another planet " line with Swedenborg, with Moses' shining face after his interview on Mount Sinai, with Schoenberg's extension of musical techniques in his endeavour to communicate the numinous. All of this—and it does not matter whether the listener knows it or not—is relevant to the visionary Priam as he beholds " the mirrored world within," and to the music which may enable us to catch a glimpse of it.

King Priam, in dramatic form, is far better disciplined than was *A Midsummer Marriage*. The acts are shapely and provide a theatrical progress which the producer, Sam Wanamaker, has most strikingly and effectively presented. The scenes of each act are linked by interludes of chorus and commentary. Tippett says he has learnt from Brecht, and Sean Kenny's ingenious set is based on the fashionable tilted disc, but with a central revolve that can whisk scenery in and out, and that also, as it reverses the slope when turned about, provides interesting variations of level. The opera is staged with imagination and skill, and will look even better on the larger stage and under the more flexible light of Covent Garden.

But—I have delayed this but as long as possible—stimulating as it is to the imagination, fertile in and productive of ideas—I still have some unresolved doubts on whether, quite simply as an opera, *King Priam* is completely effective. While watching and listening in the theatre we are inevitably concerned in the first place with the immediate action, with the characters before us; and although there were several passages of patent dramatic impact, there are others which are somewhat unconvincing—passages where Tippett's resource and skill in theatre music have failed him—which seem almost naive.

Many passages are accompanied by chamber orchestra, often by only a single line. Here Hermes' aria is uncharacteristic: a flute melody, piano chords, and harp arpeggios cradle voice, and allow every word to sound.

But when Hecuba has nothing but a single line of rushing violins to support her, and Andromache must somehow place her melody above nothing but a very elaborate cello line, and woodwind solos accompany the main Paris-Helen duet, then not only do the words tend to be hopelessly obscured (for one violin can be more obliterating than full strings), but also the singers are unaided; they have to think so much about the notes that it is hard for them to make the dramatic points properly. Yet many of the cast overcome this difficulty with astonishing success.

These are first impressions. But by the third act many of the awkwardnesses in the nature of the score seem to have sorted themselves out. A kind of Hindemithian wilfulness of counterpoint yielded to a grave, shining beauty and eloquence.

Reproduced by arrangement with The Financial Times.

A HERO OF TRAGIC STATURE

Coventry Theatre: *King Priam*

Hecuba .... MARIE COLLIER
Nurse .... NOREEN BERRY
Priam .... FORBES ROBINSON
Old Man .... DAVID KELLY
Young Guard ..... ROBERT BOWMAN
Hector .... VICTOR GODFREY
Paris .... JOHN DOBSON
Helen .... MARGRETA ELKINS
Hermes .... JOHN LANIGAN
Andromache .... JOSEPHINE VEASEY
Achilles .... RICHARD LEWIS
Patroclus .... JOSEPH WARD
Producer: SAM WANAMAKER

Designer: SEAN KENNY
Conductor: JOHN PRITCHARD
FROM OUR MUSIC CRITIC
COVENTRY, MAY 29

Michael Tippett's second opera, *King Priam*, was given its first performance tonight by Covent Garden Opera company in the Coventry Theatre as part of the cathedral festival. It must be said straightaway that the scenic realization, by Mr. Sam Wanamaker and Mr. Sean Kenny, is quite superb, vitually the most impressive opera production that this company his given us since Mr. Zeffirelli's famous *Cavalleria*. And then it must be added that the content of the opera is worthy of this magnificent spectacle.

Drama and music are not dwarfed but supported and illumined by Mr. Kenny's projections of bold, bright colour, and by the monumental masonry which appears so quietly and evokes so perfectly the heroic grandeur of the epic story—it will be seen to even greater advantage when the opera reaches Covent Garden next week.

King Priam is the story of *The Iliad* seen from the Trojan walls. Not Agamemnon nor Achilles but Troy's king is the protagonist, and the tale is made theatrically manageable by being confined to his own struggle with destiny. The theme is choice; each situation demands a decision which generates its successor until, in the end, there is no choice left. Destiny guides the final result, as she did in the beginning when Priam chose to have the infant Paris killed, but was cheated of his decision. With the death of Hector, Priam becomes a shadowy, submissive priest-figure, waiting only for the end; in these scenes of the third act Tippett, as librettist-composer, creates a moving hero a tragic stature; the character is realized with pathos and dignity in a performance of remarkable authority by Mr. Forbes Robinson.

Tippett's first opera, *A Midsummer Marriage*, was a rich, largely enigmatic, and over-elaborated nexus of symbolic imagery. The symbols in *King Priam* are much simpler and they are presented with much greater directness and sense of purpose.

Clarity has throughout been Tippett's aim, and this has led him not only to extreme economy of orchestral writing (much of the vocal music, particularly for the women, is accompanied by a single instrumental line, or by piano alone; the second act is scored without strings at all, the beginning of the third act without wind or brass) but to forms and phraseology of a startling bluntness and idiosyncrasy that only gradually reveal their flexibility and emotional power.

The vocal line is generously melodious, abounding in melisma, the musical texture generally marked by Tippett's characteristic rhythmical intricacy, sometimes quirky and nervous in effect, but most often exhilarating; the score was vividly and sonorously brought to life by the forces of Covent Garden under Mr. John Pritchard, though not without some of the ragged moments that Tippett's perilously-exposed asymmetrical patterns are fated to risk.

The whole effect is heroic, even hieratical—the Rite of Ares. We are wafted away to a remote past, not only by Tippett's libretto which is often painfully stilted and inept (yet not inappropriate for the utterances of horse-taming Hector and dazzling Achilles) but by the martial bray of brass, the opaque droning of lower strings that accompanies Priam's self-questioning, the stiff solemn tramp of procession, and the distant cries of "War!"

There are still problems of performance: the casting of the boy Paris, the choral writing, the costume and indeed the whole characterization of Hermes, and the unaccompanied ensembles of soloists which do not tell harmonically. But in sum the first performance was remarkably well cast, from home strength. Besides Mr. Robinson, special praise must be given to the Hecuba of Miss Marie Collier, the Hector of Mr. Victor Godfrey, and, particularly, the Achilles of Mr. Richard Lewis who did full justice to two landmarks in the opera, a song with guitar accompaniment (exquisitely played by Mr. John Williams), and the tremendous, frenzied war-cry with which Achilles ends the second act.

King Priam : at Coventry
by Colin Mason

MICHAEL TIPPETT'S new opera "King Priam," which had its first performance in the Coventry Theatre as part of the Cathedral Festival, last night, is as simple and clear dramatically and musically as his earlier opera "The Midsummer Marriage" was complex and tangled. The composer describes the theme of the opera as "the mysterious nature of human choice, seen in the relations between Priam, King of Troy, Hecuba his wife, his sons Hector and Paris, and their wives Andromache and Helen."

The libretto, which is his own, interprets these characters and their actions from a new point of view, and has some ingenious features which are not in any Greek original, but Tippett here resists the temptation to load his interpretation too heavily with additional meanings and associations.

In the music too he rejects the maze-like web of lyrical counterpoint of "The Midsummer Marriage," in favour of a spare, often stark texture of isolated and much more angular instrumental lines. The result is an entirely new kind of Tippettian idiom, though in other respects the musical method and personality are as unmistakably his as in the earlier opera. The orchestra is at least as important a contributor to the music drama as the singers, and some of the most striking musical invention in the work is given to the orchestra. Each main character has his own instantly identifiable and memorable theme, each cast for a certain instrument or instruments, and although there is scarcely any development of these themes in any conventional musical sense, there are many conspicuous dramatic recurrences of them. Perhaps the most telling of these is in the scene where Priam learns of Hector's death, when the first act music accompanying his d e c i s i o n whether Paris should live or die, returns under an almost identical vocal line. This great scene of grief (sung here by Forbes Robinson, with a wonderfully musical realisation of Tippett's direction to the singer to "moan") is the expressive high point of the opera and perhaps its most beautiful scene—corresponding in many ways, in the musical and dramatic scheme to the great funeral ensemble in "The Midsummer Marriage."

Elsewhere the vocal writing is not always melodically so memorable, partly because of the deliberately declamatory style, partly perhaps also because a lyrical line comes more naturally to Tippett. But in this sphere too he throws up some startlingly original and effective things, such as Achilles's war cry, the war cries of the chorus (which is off stage almost throughout the opera) and the various ensembles. These consist mainly of a series of trios into which the music periodically freezes—two for the "Greek chorus" in the interludes of act one, one for the three principal men in act 2, and the last for the three principal women in act 3. (In his use of concerted voices, as of instruments, Tippett to some extent tries to keep timbres separate rather than to blend them.)

Other first impressions of this exciting work crowd in too thickly to be got down in a hasty notice. But two that should be mentioned are the arresting originality and effectiveness of the brass writing in the military (and hunting) music and the magnificent curtain-falls to the first two acts: the Judgment of Paris for the first, ending in his being cursed by Athene and Hera, in the persons of Hecuba and Andromache, for his choice of Aphrodite in the person of Helen (which is also musically one of the opera's great moments); and for the second the thrilling off-stage war cry of the approaching Achilles, roused at last by the death of Patroclus to enter the fighting.

Tippett is fortunate, as he was in "The Midsummer Marriage" equally in the imaginatively simple and masterly production by Sam Wanamaker, on a steeply raked circular stage, and in the noble costumes and the beautiful and ingenious set by Sean Kenny. He was well served also by his singers, above all by Forbes Robinson in the part of King Priam, which is in every sense the greatest in the work. Among the other men Victor Godfrey as Hector and John Dobson as Paris sang well, though they were eclipsed by Richard Lewis and John Lanigan in the smaller "character" tenor parts of Achilles and Hermes. Hecuba and Andromache, both cast as highly articulate and intelligent women, were both excellently sung by Marie Collier and Josephine Veasey (Miss Veasey made hers sound the most sensuously written vocal part in the work), while the fairly thankless part of Helen, one of the dumbest blondes ever to walk the operatic stage, was self-sacrificingly undertaken by Margreta Elkins. John Pritchard directed them all, and the Covent Garden orchestra and chorus in a performance of impressive authority and assurance all round.

The Knot Garden

Tippett's subliminal sex drama

The Knot Garden
Covent Garden
William Mann

Michael Tippett's third opera, given its first performance last night at Covent Garden, has been much publicized as an epoch-making new production, first-fruit of the Peter Hall-Colin Davis duumvirate which will take control of the Royal Opera next autumn. The result is visibly and audibly impressive.

The new opera has been cast, not from domestic strength (few Covent Garden regular principal singers have been under annual contract in recent years) but from young actor-singers who are right for these particular roles—several of them, though already well-known elsewhere, were making their debuts in the Royal Opera House. Mr. Hall's production is unusually striking, too, by British operatic standards, though its blend of visible stage spaciousness and confined, intimate acting area is familiar elsewhere.

Much can be said about the performance, not merely that it makes a good evening in the theatre for people who would not dream of looking at *Il Trovatore* or *Figaro* or even *Peter Grimes* as presently staged. Just now the only important topic is *The Knot Garden* and what sort of an opera it is.

On the surface it may appear to be a domestic country-house comedy about well-to-do people with problems. But Tippett, though well familiar with N. C. Hunter and T. S. Eliot characters, goes farther, confuses their gracious living by introducing other people unsuitable in such plays and, because music is his chief expressive medium, causes them all to express inner feelings and desires that are naturally music's province, yet for him also need to be externalized in words which you and I might conceivably imagine but would never say.

The most outspoken scene is the one where Faber, the ultra-respectable businessman, dark suit, briefcase, emblem of respectability, obviously innocent of designs on his teenage female ward, makes advances to a young homosexual musician. On stage, with Raimund Herincx as tycoon, the whole idea is absurd—but curiouser designs have been nurtured by outwardly boring people.

Most immediately striking, and most suitable for opera, is the entry of the maquis-girl Denise. Until her arrival the opera has been conducted in declamatory recitative and personal introduction. Then she walks on, physically deformed, hideously disfigured about the face, unnaturally thin, and bursts into a long solo aria, very florid, intense, loud (how can slim Josephine Barstow unleash so much searing, not to mention accurate and unforced, volume?). Denise reveals all her recollections of the torture she has suffered. Nobody in life or in a play would do this, in company—let alone in the reposeful, ordered garden of a country-house. Denise does, and in this operatic drama it is necessary and right. We are thereby prepared for the second act in which the drama is taken over by psychological strip-tease of this sort.

Tippett wants us to watch psychological development, the frankness that brings about self-knowledge: but opera for him involves magic and so the gradual resolution of the several characters' many conflicts is brought about by unfair psycho-analytical tricks. Mangus, the psycho-analyst, admits eventually that he is a fake (they are all faking to some extent) and his therapy, at first by precipitating many duet confrontations, then by organizing a charade that goes wrong (right for self-knowledge), helps only the older husband and wife, who end by coming durably together—we are asked to believe. The other persons go away with a million problems on their shoulders, especially the two who have shown themselves the most worthwhile and interesting, the teenage ward Flora, only just free of her Peter Pan cocoon, and the unwilling, gentle, mixed up queer Dov.

I can't believe in this ending. The composer regards it as an open end, because persons go on developing until they die. But since music formalizes human response on stage (and this opera includes formalized solos and ensembles of devastating impact and inventive quality), the drama ought to formalize as well. It doesn't, because life doesn't. We are asked to imagine what happens afterwards. In one case Tippett has written the sequel, the *Songs for Dov*, an admirable piece; but when is Flora's song-cycle? How helpful is it that Mel went off with Denise—the worst-assorted couple in history, surely?

We will go on making comments of this kind, just because the characters have become real, identifiable, by the end of the opera. Not through their words (stilted, often mercifully inaudible, pegs for good music), partly through the vitality of their personifications, most cogently through Tippett's music which is violent, discreet, bitter and deeply loving, brilliant and satirical—not always in expected contexts. The Blues ensemble at the end of the first act arises from polite reaction and is voiced unrealistically, yet it works well enough to drain the blood from your cheeks.

The Knot Garden is strong enough to provoke comment of all sorts for as long as any theatre can find time to present it—it must be revived soon and regularly at Covent Garden with this and other casts. Colin Davis's conducting at this première blazed with authenticity. In this cast Thomas Hemsley's analyst, Robert Tear's lonely musician, Jill Gomez's teenager (perhaps too sophisticated), and Josephine Barstow's Denise won special respect. The opera won me most of all because the whole cast, and the production, operated as an ensemble, a human mechanism working together, something rare in opera. The labyrinth in Act II, should move more busily, but otherwise the production looks tremendous. The chorus placed in the audience at the end is a dramatic coup, that may work once but not at the umpteenth revival to which I look forward.

Six people's fantasies in new Tippett opera

By MARTIN COOPER

IN his new opera "The Knot Garden," which had its first performance at Covent Garden last night, Sir Michael Tippett returns to the theme of his "Midsummer Marriage" — human relationships and the development of the individual psyche.

While in the earlier opera he drew the symbol of his libretto from primitive rituals, now he places his characters in a maze, or labyrinth, whose shifting shapes reflect the lability of their personalities.

Directed by a fatherly analyst, six immature or stunted people are made to act out the fantasies of their inner lives in an attempt to grow up.

A childless couple and their girl ward, a freedom-fighting woman, and two "gay" boys engage in a kind of group therapy, which enables each to exteriorise private fantasies or promptings of attraction and repulsion, in fleeting scenes of overt violence or tenderness.

This is, in fact, an expressionistic drama "in depth," and aimed (clearly for audience as well as cast) at general catharsis, or at least preliminary clearing of decks, rather than the solution of individual problems.

★

The listener's engagement was greatly facilitated by Peter Hall's resourceful stage-production, unusually closely integrated with the music, and Timothy O'Brien's imaginative set of revolving aluminium rods, forming a kinetic labyrinth.

With Colin Davis conducting, this production shows a singleness of aim that has hardly been matched in opera here since Tippett's own "King Priam."

If the new opera is designed as a total theatrical experience, Tippett's music remains the factor by which it will ultimately be judged. Perhaps with the potentially wider public of musical theatre—rather than opera —in mind, he has filled his score with an extraordinary variety of attractions.

Much of the music consists of gestures—brass fanfares and percussive cannonades of explosions—whose primary function is theatrical, but there are some set-pieces that will stand comparison with the best things in the earlier operas.

It is characteristic that the climactic finale of Act I is a big ensemble based on a blues rhythm initiated by the Negro writer Mel (Thomas Carey) and designed to release the tension created by a long aria, in which the freedom-fighter, Denise, evokes the horrors of torture and imprisonment.

As the only character centred on an objective ideal outside herself, Denise easily dominates the work by the directness and stark seriousness of her music, in which florid vocalisation and trills are put to heroic instead of decorative use and were sung with superb intensity and technical mastery by Josephine Barstow.

The decorative element is strong in Flora's music, sung with charming grace and skill by Jill Gomez.

A more fantastic kind of music, full of self-mockery and parody, is given to Dov (Robert Tear) and seems to forecast his eventual exclusion from the final pattern.

★

In the welter of cross-relating symbols, the "Tempest" analogy, which runs through the work, is pressed so closely in Act III that its fundamental irrelevance seemed to me clear. It provided Thomas Hemsley, however, with an effective Prospero-mask for his analyst, Mangus.

Both Yvonne Minton and Raimund Herincx sang with great force and distinction as Thea and Faber, but this childless mother-woman and adolescent-minded business man were the least convincing of the characters, and I find it difficult to credit their final reconciliation.

These, however, are incidental blemishes on a work which is a triumphant example of musical theatre concerning itself with genuinely human values.

94

Sydney Edwards

at the

first night

of Tippett's

new opera

Up the garden path

THERE were several moments in Sir Michael Tippett's opera The Knot Garden, given its premiere at Covent Garden last night, when one of the characters went down on all fours and barked: " Bow - wow - wow " for no particular reason. And there was also the homosexual in pink socks and suede shoes, plus the wife who took a whip to her husband. At last Covent Garden has arrived in the 20th-century !

Then there was 20th century language like " Stop the world I want to get off . . . We shall overcome . . . Take the mickey out of me . . . Baby, don't torment me."

All designed to prove to our consciences and to the rest of the world that the Royal Opera House is now where it is at. But in this particular garden you cannot see the wood for the trees. The opera's music and particularly the production have many outstanding points but the use of conventional, stereotyped characters and out-of-date language are flaws.

The seven people in the cast are almost unbelievable but un-

fortunately the opera is about their characters and their loves and hates. The action takes place in a garden and especially in the knot-garden of the title. Knot-gardens were intricate, formal patterns in Elizabethan gardens. The opera analyses the difficulties of seven people relating to each other in the " knot-garden " of the modern world.

In the first act the seven meet and set up tensions between each other. In the second they reveal their " inner selves " and in the third act all is apparently resolved.

Tippett offers us varying emotions and attempts insight by several means including a charade in which five of the characters assume roles from The Tempest.

But the resolutions of the last act are far from clear and the device of audience participation (a chorus scattered in the audience throughout the house) was more irritating than effective.

However, the opera is, I suppose, a brave attempt to bring modern people onto the stage.

The music is always intriguing and stimulating. The orchestra-

tion is quite superb and the moods run from the blues to Schubert.

As a production The Knot Garden is one of the most integrated and brilliant Covent Garden has ever staged. Peter Hall in the manner of his production of A Delicate Balance groups the seven conflicting characters in the most telling ways and has done his considerable best to bring them alive as people.

The set of glimmering trees by Timothy O'Brien and lit by John Bury is visually the most stunning to be seen in London.

Colin Davis, who conducted, has obviously prepared the work with the greatest of love and care. The seven singers could not be faulted. There were excellent performances by Raimund Herincx, Yvonne Minton, Jill Gomez, Josephine Barstow, Thomas Carey, Robert Tear and Thomas Hemsley.

One looks forward to future revivals. Perhaps the characters and their problems will become clearer on closer acquaintance. But at the moment a psychiatrist with a black beard and a homosexual in suede shoes do little to convince me of reality.

Sir Michael's maze

Philip Hope-Wallace reviews 'The Knot Garden' at Covent Garden

SIR MICHAEL TIPPETT'S new opera "The Knot Garden," was given a first and beautifully presented performance at Covent Garden on Wednesday under Colin Davis. It will be broadcast tomorrow. A subtitle to this deeply intriguing work of art might be "All in a Maze." "Pleased but puzzled" might sum up an average reaction. The new set-up at the Royal Opera believes that it is the kind of work to coax a new and "wider" audience. I wonder. The anomaly can hardly be ignored, however, that whereas a new ballet has the ballet public stampeding for seats, from a new opera it is precisely the opera public which stays away.

It is no use pretending that this work is easy, or instantly accessible, delivering instant rewards. It is claimed that the music illumines a libretto which textually reminds me rather of some play by Auden and Isherwood in the thirties. For some, this consummation devoutly to be wished may occur. For me as yet, not. That lie : familiarity breeds contempt needs nailing. Familiarity can breed love and understanding. My prayer is that I shall come to know and like this score as much as, over the years, I have come to understand a once baffling work "The Midsummer Marriage."

But here, at curtain fall, I can say two things : Timothy O'Brien's scenery is the most lovesome operatic garden I have looked on : ombrageous back projections, a tracery of transparent hanging rods (on the move in the Maze scenes). Second, that you don't have to hear ten minutes before realising that this is not a fashionable confection "from the head" but a score of deep feeling and meaning—from the heart.

The story is no more arcane or impractical for operatic treatment than "Die Frau Ohne Schatten." It is also something akin to "Cosi Fan Tutte" in that a clutch of people, pair by pair, come to a new understanding of their relationships, under the hand of a wise magician (modernly, a psychiatrist) who, looking like David Low, puts this knot of tied up souls through a final charade of "The Tempest," used as what the scientologists call "dianetics." Strife and cacophony yield to new pairings, calmer duets, healed resolutions. A beautiful theme, I think.

Thomas Hemsley is the modern dress Prospero. The couples involved are a warring pair of spouses (Mr Herincx and Miss Minton, superb both) ; Flora their ward in the throes of adolescence and Denise, a shrill freedom fighter (Jill Gomez and Josephine Barstow, again splendid) and a male homosexual couple—black Mel (Thomas Carey) and white tenor Dov (Robert Tear). The action physical consists of encounters, largely duets in a Maze, followed in act three (short, about 30 minutes music each) by the Tempest analogy, quotes from "These yellow sands," echoed by voices planted in the auditorium and "leave not a wrack behind."

The hinge of the musico-dramatic idea seemed to me to be the duet between Flora and Dov which merges out of her quoting Schubert's "Mein Schatz hat Grün so gern" flowering into a duet which is instantly beautiful, but seemed to me too long, relatively speaking. I think Tippett's sense of operatic length is sometimes defective. Thea the wife and gardening enthusiast also has a solo scena, which is clearly a most eloquent moment—though I couldn't hope to reproduce a bar of it in my memory—but then I can't say that "King Priam" even actually sings in my head. This is, I fear, where I remain an outsider.

A mimic, of some skill generally, I find that while I recall many shimmering, colourful, dramatic, exciting or consoling comments from the orchestral pit, hardly a single vocal phrase (except those where the characters drop into speech) has etched itself on my memory. Indeed at the time, this vocal line sounded to my unreceptive ear to be arbitrary in the sense that it seemed strangely immaterial on which note the singer's voice next alighted. No question of anticipating and being proved less happy in one guess than the composer. Simply a feeling that a phrase might take almost any shape at will, not memorable and meaningful, but like the word sequences of Gertrude Stein.

Where the diction came through clearly of course one received the message, but for me the vocalisation did not illumine the thought. I make so damaging an admission in preference to pretending (which is bad criticism). People thought as much about Pélléas once. I expect time will show my error. Meanwhile, it is short, pithy, totally un-boring. The second act, if not the third, will probably hold you completely. Also it is piquant. The baritone (Husband) gets a whipping from his wife and then gets a kiss from the queer Dov (tenor). I thought in the interval that the marble busts of Patti and Melba in the foyer exchanged affronted glances. "Opera duets weren't like that in our day." No indeed. But there is a palpable magic coming off the stage here all the same. Sample it.

Reproduced by arrangement with The Guardian.

Startling stuff from the new whizz kids

THE KNOT GARDEN
Royal Opera

A DEFIANT challenge to opera convention was hurled from the Covent Garden stage last night by Colin Davis and Peter Hall, who become joint directors of the Royal Opera next year.

They are the conductor and producer respectively of Sir Michael Tippett's third opera, which was loudly and deservedly cheered after its premiere.

The composer has again written his own libretto, involving seven characters of today whose personalities and problems impinge on one another in the knot garden of their characters.

In the first act they meet and set up tensions. In the second they expose their inner selves one to another. The last act achieves a resolution of sorts.

This act remains the most problematical in an otherwise stunning and inventive production that is a theatrical experience on its own, with the aid of brilliantly original stage design by Timothy O'Brien.

Nerves

Emotions and the nerve-ends of individual personality are conveyed less by the words than by the music, which adds clarity of line and subtlety of colour to Tippett's always lush invention.

At the same time, it has not entirely solved the problem of getting all crucial words across.

The cast is nevertheless a generally fine one. Josephine Barstow makes much of Denise, a "freedom-fighter" with an arm withered and a face searingly scarred by torture, whose arrival is the spark to the inflammable secret selves of the rest.

These include Robert Tear and the Negro Thomas Carey as Dov and Mel, musician and writer, locked in a homosexual tangle of their own.

Raimund Herincx and Yvonne Minton are an engineer and his wife, at odds with each other but finally reconciled — two forthright portraits, like that of Jill Gomez as a somewhat too sophisticated Flora, a young girl afraid of growing up.

It is an opera that should give even opera-haters much to enjoy—and more to think about.

Reproduced by arrangement with The Daily Express.

America

Over the last twelve years, Michael Tippett has developed a special sense of kinship with America. Oddly enough, he hadn't even been there until 1965, when he was invited to the Aspen Festival as composer-in-residence. Indeed, before the war, he had been almost actively opposed to going to the USA and working there, as did Britten, Auden, Isherwood &c: though, in any case, he had no means of earning a living there. He was aware of jazz, which he loved, and of the literary flowering that had occurred in New England before and after the Civil War, with Whitman and others. Nevertheless, he felt that he himself, and the compositions he was then writing, like *A Child of Our Time*, belonged — despite the presence of Negro Spirituals — within the European world.

Some time later, he met Aaron Copland in London. Copland told him he'd heard Tippett's *Concerto for Double String Orchestra* by accident, and had thought it was a piece of American music. This triggered off something in Tippett's mind. It was not long afterwards that he went to Aspen, and he says that it was as if he had arrived in his own private Mayflower. Aspen was not New England, but it was his first contact with a polyglot culture that made a deep impression upon him. He has responded equally, ever since, to the extraordinary contrasts provided by Spanish America and the Indians; the curious culture of the Pacific coast cities; the different races and creeds; the skyscrapers of New York and Chicago: and the natural landscapes produced by erosion of red rock and sandstone in Monument Valley, Utah.

The bare facts of Tippett's subsequent involvement with America are easily stated. He has been back there often, to conduct various orchestras — including the Chicago Symphony Orchestra in 1974, in a performance of his *Third Symphony* — and attend performances of some of his major works – such as the American premiere of *The Knot Garden* at Northwestern University, Evanston, Illinois. The Chicago Orchestra has also commissioned his recently completed Fourth Symphony, which Sir Georg Solti will conduct in October 1977. In 1976, he gave the Doty Lectures in Fine Art at the University of Austin, Texas. Tippett is also an Honorary Member of the American Academy of Arts and Letters. In America now, his music has become widely popular. Students have been seen at concerts wearing sweaters bearing the slogan "Turn On To Tippett"!

But what has happened in the last twelve years is that Tippett has felt the desire to live emotionally within America. He has read American history and steeped himself in its literature and culture generally. His view of Europe is now, consequently, rather different. Naturally, the spill-off in his musical work has been considerable. *The Ice Break*, most of all, reflects this newfound land of the spirit.

Meirion Bowen 1977

Miscellaneous

Tues. I've been meaning to tell
you that, in Zambia, the alto solo
at a rehearsal confused her
consonants & sang: "But the
soul, watching the chaotic mirror,
knews that the Sods return".
A marvellous emendation!

M

106

109

Dear Richard with love from Ben 1965

Benjamin Britten

Curlew River

A PARABLE FOR CHURCH PERFORMANCE

Op. 71

Libretto based on the medieval Japanese Nō-play
Sumidagawa of Jūrō Motomasa (1395-1431)

by WILLIAM PLOMER

German translation by Ludwig Landgraf
Rehearsal Score by Imogen Holst
Production Notes by Colin Graham

FABER AND FABER LIMITED
24 Russell Square London

Sole Agents for USA: G. Schirmer, Inc., New York

May 4, 1977   Wed.

    Good news. The Dallas Symphony Orchestra has agreed to perform
some music by Michael during the 77-78 season. This came about
this past weekend when we broadcast a 56-hour marathon program
to raise money for the symphony. One of the incentives given to
donors to the Dallas Symphony Orch. was that whoever won the
popularity contest among composers - the DSO would perform one
of their works during the upcoming season. Mahler got off to an
early lead followed by Beethoven, but it wasn't long until the
active support given over the air by Stephen and myself brought
Tippett into the lead to stay despite several close calls. You see
if someone gave $35 to the DSO they could have 35 votes for their
favorite composer. In the end Michael came out ahead, so now the
DSO management has agreed to program some of his music.
    I'll keep you informed on any further decisions concerning
the playing of Michael's music by the DSO. It's very exciting
for us here - at least for the Dallas Chapter of the Tippett
Fan Club which has been growing for the past several years.

                    Sincerely,

                    Victor Marshall
                    Victor Marshall

                    _____
                    Extract from a letter to Schott & Co. London

Honours

1959	CBE
1966	KBE

Honorary Doctorates

1964	University of Cambridge
1964	Trinity College, Dublin
1965	University of Leeds
1966	University of York
1967	University of Oxford
1968	University of Leicester
1968	University of Wales
1970	University of Bristol
1972	University of Bath
1974	University of Warwick
1975	University of London
1976	University of Sheffield
1976	University of Birmingham
1977	University of Lancaster

1961	Fellow of Royal College of Music
1976	Elected Honorary member of American Academy of Arts and Letters.
1976	Elected extraordinary member of the Akademie der Künste Berlin.
1976	Gold Medal Royal Philharmonic Society.

Manuscripts

The following scores are in public collections.

Concerto for Piano & Orchestra	Ink ms.	Barber Institute
King Priam	Pencil ms.	Library of Congress
King Priam	Ink ms.	British Library
The Knot Garden	Pencil ms.	Northwestern University USA
The Midsummer Marriage	Pencil ms.	British Library
Severn Bridge Variation (Braint)	Ink ms.	B.B.C.
String Quartet no. 1 (original version)	Ink ms.	British Library
Suite for the Birthday of Prince Charles	Ink ms.	B.B.C.

The following scores are in private collections.

Divertimento on 'Sellenger's Round' Mvts 1 & 2	Ink ms.
Lullaby	Ink ms.
Songs for Achilles nos. 1 & 2	Ink ms.
Songs for Ariel & 'Tempest' music	Pencil ms.
Songs for Dov	Pencil ms.
Wadhurst	Ink ms.

N.B. Most compositions exist in 2 versions, a preliminary pencil score and the final 'Ink' copy.

It is possible that this above listing is not complete, if details are known of any other works in collections the publishers would be grateful for information concerning them.

Recordings of works by Michael Tippett

78rpm recordings:—

Non commercial discs

1941   Fantasy Sonata for Piano — Phyllis Sellick
        Recorded by Decca for Rimington Van Wyck Ltd.
        2 double sided and one single sided 12" records

1944   Concerto for Double String Orchestra
        Orchestra conducted by Walter Goehr
        Recorded by Levy Sound Studios for Schott & Co. Ltd.
        3 Double sided 12" records

Commercial recordings

1948   String Quartet No. 2 — Zorian Quartet
        3 double sided 12" records   DECCA AK 1925-7

1952   Concerto for Double String Orchestra
        Philharmonia Orch. cond. Walter Goehr
        3 double sided 12" records   HMV C7926-8

33⅓rpm recordings:
All recordings stereo except where marked ⓜ which denotes mono

1953   Boyhoods End
        The Hearts Assurance
        Peter Pears, Noel Mewton-Wood   ARGO ⓜ RG 15

1953   Lament on 'Sellengers Round' from
        'Variations on an Elizabethan Theme'
        Aldeburgh Festival Orch. cond. Benjamin Britten   DECCA ⓜ LXT 2798

1953   Dance, Clarion Air from
        'A Garland for the Queen'
        Golden Age Singers, Cambridge University
        Musical Society cond. Boris Ord   COLUMBIA ⓜ 33CX 1063

1955   Concerto for Double String Orchestra
        Philharmonia Orch. cond. Walter Goehr
        L.P. transfer of 1952 78 rpm recording   HMV ⓜ CLP 1056

1956   String Quartet No. 2
        Amadeus Quartet   HMV ⓜ ALP 1302

1958   A Child of Our Time
        Morrison, Bowden, Lewis, Standen
        Royal Liverpool Philharmonic Orch. and Choir
        cond. John Pritchard

        coupled with

        Ritual Dances from The Midsummer Marriage
        Orch. of Royal Opera House, Covent Garden
        cond. John Pritchard   PYE ⓜ 30114/5

1960   Sonata No. 1 for Piano
        Margaret Kitchin   LYRITA ⓜ RCS 5

1963   Magnificat and Nunc Dimittis
        St. John's College Choir cond. George Guest   ARGO ⓜ RG340
                                                          ZRG 5340

1963	Concerto for Double String Orchestra Bath Festival Orch., Moscow Chamber Orch. cond. Rudolf Barshai	HMV (m) ALP 1961 ASD 512
1963	A Child of Our Time c/w Ritual Dances re-issue of 1958 recording With stereo release new	ARGO (m) DA 19/20 ZDA 19/20
1965	Concerto for Orchestra London Symphony Orchestra cond. Colin Davis	PHILIPS (m) AL 3497 SAL 3497
1965	Concerto for Piano and Orchestra John Ogdon, Philharmonia Orchestra cond. Colin Davis c/w Sonata No. 2 for Piano John Ogdon	HMV (m) ALP 2073 ASD 621
1965	Fantasia Concertante on a Theme of Corelli Bath Festival Orch. cond. composer	HMV (m) ALP 2090 ASD 637
1965	Songs for Ariel Peter Pears, Benjamin Britten	ARGO (m) RG 439 ZRG 5439
1965	String Quartet No. 2 — Amadeus Quartet re-issue of 1956 recording c/w Boyhoods End and The Hearts Assurance Peter Pears and Noel Mewton-Wood re-issue of 1953 recording	ARGO (m) DA 34
1965	String Quartet No. 1	WAVERLEY (m) LLP 1027 SLLP 1028
1965	Preludio al Vespro di Monteverdi Paul Morgan. Exeter Cathedral organ	EXON EAS 18
1966	Early one morning The Elizabethan Singers	ARGO (m) RG 496 ZRG 5496
1967	Concerto for Double String Orchestra Philharmonia Orch. cond.. Walter Goehr re-issue of 1955 transfer	MUSIC FOR PLEASURE (m) MFP 2069
1967	Sonata No. 1 for Piano John Ogdon	HMV ASD 2321/2
1967	String Quartet No. 1 String Quartet No. 3 — Fidelio Quartet	PYE (m) GGC 4079 GSGC 14079
1967	Sonata No. 2 for Piano Peter Cooper	PYE (m) GGC 4085 GSGC 14085
1967	Preludio al Vespro di Monteverdi Simon Preston	ARGO (m) RG 528 ZRG 528

1968	Symphony No. 2 London Symphony Orch. cond. Colin Davis c/w Sonata for 4 Horns — B. Tuckwell Horn Quartet c/w The Weeping Babe — John Alldis Choir	ARGO ⓜ RG 535 ZRG 535
1968	Suite for the Birthday of Prince Charles (Suite in D) Leicestershire Schools Symphony Orch. cond. composer	PYE ⓜ GGC 4103 GSGC 14103
1968	Songs for Achilles No. 1 In the Tent: 'O rich soiled land' Richard Lewis, John Williams, guitar	DECCA ⓜ MET 392/3 SET 392/2
1969	Concerto for Double String Orchestra Bath Festival Orch. Moscow Chamber Orch. cond. Rudolf Barshai re-issue of 1963 release	WORLD RECORD CLUB ⓜ T829 ST 829
1970	String Quartet No. 2 — Fidelio Quartet	PYE GSGC 14130
1971	Interlude 2 and Epilogue from The Shires Suite Leicestershire Schools Symphony Orch. cond. composer	ARGO ZRG 685
1971	The Midsummer Marriage Soloists, Chorus and Orch. of the Royal Opera House, Covent Garden cond. Colin Davis	PHILIPS 6703 027
1972	Concerto for Double String Orchestra Fantasia Concertante on a theme of Corelli Little Music for Strings Academy of St. Martins in the Fields cond. Neville Marriner	ARGO ZRG 680
1972	The Vision of St. Augustine John Shirley-Quirk, London Symphony Orch. and Chorus cond. composer c/w Fantasia on a Theme of Handel Margaret Kitchin, London Symphony Orch. cond. composer	RCA SER 5620
1972	5 Negro Spirituals No. 4 from BBC TV series 'Songs of Praise'	B.B.C. REC 141
1973	Songs for Ariel No. 3 'Where the bee sucks' Simon Woolf, Steuart Bedford	UNICORN UNS 236
1973	Songs for Dov Robert Tear, London Sinfonietta cond. David Atherton	ARGO ZRG 703
1973	Concerto for Double String Orchestra Bath Festival Orch. Moscow Chamber Orch. cond. Rudolf Barshai re-issue of 1963 recording	HMV CONCERT CLASSICS SXLP 30157

1974	The Knot Garden Soloists and Orch. of the Royal Opera House, Covent Garden, cond. Colin Davis	PHILIPS 6700 063
1974	Concerto for Double String Orchestra London Philharmonic Orch. cond. Vernon Handley	CLASSICS FOR PLEASURE CFP 40068
1974	5 Negro Spirituals Canterbury Cathedral Choir cond. Allan Wicks	GROSVENOR GRO 1034
1974	Sonatas for Piano Nos. 1, 2, 3 Paul Crossley	PHILIPS 6500 534
1975	Dance, Clarion Air Plebs Angelica Canterbury Cathedral Choir cond. Allan Wicks	GROSVENOR GRS 1030
1975	Concerto for Orchestra London Symphony Orch. cond. Colin Davis re-issue of 1965 recording c/w Ritual Dances from complete recording of Midsummer Marriage of 1971 **Not** the concert version	PHILIPS 6580 093
1975	A Child of Our Time Norman, Baker, Cassilly, Shirley-Quirk BBC Singers, Choral Soc. and Orch. cond. Colin Davis	PHILIPS 6500 985
1975	String Quartets Nos. 1-3 Lindsay Quartet	L'OISEAU LYRE DSLO 10
1975	Fantasia Concertante on a Theme of Corelli c/w Little Music for Strings Orchestra of St. Johns Smith Square cond. John Lubbock	PYE TPLS 13069
1975	Symphony No. 3 Harper, London Symphony Orch. cond. Colin Davis	PHILIPS 6500 662
1976	5 Negro Spirituals Leeds Parish Church Choir cond. Donald Hunt	ABBEY LPB 754
1976	Symphony No. 1 Suite for the Birthday of Prince Charles London Symphony Orch. cond. Colin Davis	PHILIPS 9500 107
1976	Boyhoods End The Hearts Assurance Songs for Ariel Songs for Achilles* Philip Langridge, John Constable Piano *Timothy Walker Guitar	L'OISEAU LYRE DSLO 14
1976	5 Negro Spirituals Nos. 1 and 3 Canterbury Cathedral Choir With organ acc. Philip Moore organ cond. Allan Wicks	ABBEY LPB 739
1977	A Child of Our Time c/w Ritual Dances re-issue of 1958/1963 recording	ARGO DPA 571/2

1977	Fanfare no. 1	
	Locke Brass Consort cond. James Stobart	RCA RL 25081
1977	Dance, Clarion Air from 'A Garland for the Queen'	
	Exultate Singers cond. Garrett O'Brien	RCA GL 25062
1977	Concerto for Piano and Orchestra	
	Re-issue of 1965 recording	HMV SLS 5080

Recordings of overseas manufacture

Little Music for Strings
C.B.C. Vancouver Chamber Orch.
cond. John Avison

CANADIAN BROADCASTING
CORPORATION SM 124

String Quartet No. 2
Carl Pini Quartet

AUSTRALIAN HMV SOXLP 7552

Compiled by Alan Woolgar

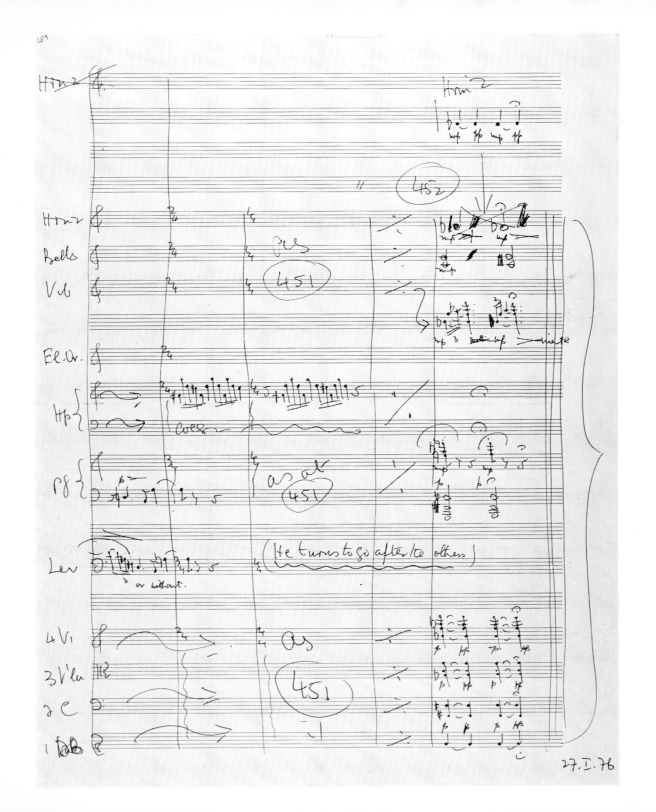

Deep within me, I know that part of the artist's job is to renew our sense of the comely and the beautiful. To create a dream. Every human being has this need to dream. It might seem that this need is satisfied by the simplicities of popular art but behind the mass demand for entertainment lies somewhere the desire for something more permanent, for the deeper satisfaction of proportion and beauty in a world of impersonal exploitation — a world which has no care for the inner person. And if for the poet this means a barren age what does he mean by 'barren'? Our age is not technologically barren. Technology means power and vast production through machines. So man can apparently accomplish everything for good or ill. He can produce abundance, he can manufacture milk powder for starving children in vast quantities. Technology has potentially all the answers for a hungry world.

The barrenness of the age lies in the deprivation of man's imaginative life once he has put all value into machines. As man becomes more and more capable scientifically, the debasement of the world of imagination produces human beings who find it harder to use decently the material abundance thus provided.

Technology has produced such huge extensions to our means of communication that as we look at photos of the starving and the dead of Bangladesh we are moved — through newspapers and television we are moved more often and more widely. Although we cannot accept that all men really will be brothers we perhaps know more about what being brothers means, because we have seen and understood the opposite. We are acutely aware of what it means to be human.

When I look at the exuberance of young people today I see the paradox between the precision and accuracy and power of the scientific world and the primitive, uncouth, even psychedelic nature of the world of popular art at its sharpest. I think the universality of this psychedelic craving is a symptom of an acutely felt imbalance in our society, an imbalance which denies the needs of the impoverished raw world of the inner self.

There are other dreams — apparently political, often incoherent. As in my youth, it is the prerogative of young men to shout for a better world. The outstanding feature of this unrest today is its universality. The outbreaks of student protest all over the world have perhaps less to do with any specific political issues than with a widespread impatience with a society that appears to have little time for dreams.

Martin Luther King said: 'I have a dream. I have a dream that my four little children will one day live in a nation where they will not be judged by the colour of their skin but by the content of their character.'

The dream is broken, as it is time and time again. The dream of the French Revolution, of the British Empire, of the 'War to end War', of the communist's Utopia. Most resounding of all for our time — Jefferson's dream of an America which accepts that all men are created equal. That dream is broken. But must I stop singing, like Hölderlin, because of the fragility of all aspiration? I do not think this is what happens. We celebrate — even in outdated forms at time, because we must. The young people who sing that great hymn of affirmation, Blake's 'Jerusalem', are not so naive as to imagine that they will in fact build it any more than that all mankind will be brothers. Yet there is a momentary vision of a possibility. The illusion we have now to discard is that this Jerusalem is still to be found outside, somewhere among the glittering promises of technology. As they leave the earth, the astonauts see it from afar — flat, round, nothing so small as a man to be seen. And that flattened out picture of the earth has always seemed to me to symbolize the devaluation of the singular, minute, particular man we all are. But I am still me on the earth and the astronaut is still one particular man on his moon. And it's my task as an artist to talk to him, to find some way to speak through the space suit of the technological man to the imaginative man within.

If art in our time seems to be standing on its head, taking on peculiar and even perverse forms, screaming in order to get attention, it's because it has been searching for the new languages we need if we are to speak to the millions of the modern world. It seems as though we've come to a point in our long history where value is returning to the world within.

Our faith in progress through technics is less absolute and because the hunger for this inner world is so alive in all of us and because this is the world the artist speaks immediately to, for the first time since the Renaissance it seems the time may be coming when the artist is once more at one with his society.

I have been writing music for forty years. During those years there have been huge and world-shattering events in which I have been inevitably caught up. Whether society has felt music valuable or needful I have gone on writing because I must. And I know that my true function within a society which embraces all of us, is to continue an age-old tradition, fundamental to our civilization, which goes back into pre-history and will go forward into the unknown future. This tradition is to create images from the depths of the imagination and to give them form whether visual, intellectual or musical. For it is only through images that the inner world communicates at all. Images of the past, shapes of the future. Images of vigour for a decadent period, images of calm for one too violent. Images of reconciliation for worlds torn by division. And in an age of mediocrity and shattered dreams, images of abounding, generous, exuberant beauty

Acknowledgements

The following are thanked for their contributions and help.

John Amis
Arts Council of Great Britain
R & J Balding Books, Edinburgh
Bath Festival
Black Star Publishing Company
Meirion Bowen
British Broadcasting Corporation
British Institute of Recorded Sound
Trustees of Britten-Pears Library
Humphrey Burton
Caligraving Limited, Thetford
Colin Davis
Lord Drogheda
William Drummond
The Gramophone
Sir Charles Groves
Peter Hall
Hansom Books
Barbara Hepworth Estate
Hulton Picture Library
Ibbs and Tillett
Ian Kemp
Commander Peter Kemp
Ralph Koltai
Sir Jack Lyons

Victor Marshall
David Matthews
Stella Maude
Sir Robert Mayer
Mechanical Copyright Protection Society
Morley College
National Press
News Chronicle
Timothy O'Brien
Phonogram, London
Photographic Services Limited
Royal College of Music, London
Royal Opera House, Covent Garden
Schott and Company, London
B. Schott Söhne, Mainz, Germany
Mrs. Frank Stokes
M. A. Tredwell
Sir Michael Tippett
Eric Walter White
Welsh National Opera
Reverend Woodbridge
Alan Woolgar

Every effort has been made to trace the possible owners of copyright material, if ommissions have been made the publishers wish to apologise.

Special thanks are due to Amina Harris for collecting the material; Betty Scholar for her extensive secretarial work; Schott and Company London for providing this handsome book.

The organisers are indebted to Keith Cheetham for the design of the exhibition and this book, and to Rick Wentworth for his close collaboration. Without their dedicated work this venture would not have been possible.

Keith Cheetham and Rick Wentworth wish to thank the Staff of Caligraving, Schott and Company, Alan Woolgar and Sally Groves for their patience, advice and hard work.

*Schott congratulate
the organising committee
on its exhibition and, as
Sir Michael Tippett's publishers,
are proud of their long
association with the
composer and his music*

The music of Michael Tippett is published exclusively by

48 Great Marlborough Street, London W1V 2BN : 01-437 1246-8

EULENBURG BOOKS

General Editor · Sir William Glock

Launched in the Eulenburg centenary year (1874-1974), this new
series of books on music follows and supplements the scholarly
pattern set by the famous Eulenburg pocket scores. The series
includes newly commissioned works on outstanding modern
musical figures, re-issues of worthwhile books too long out
of print, and translations of important French and
German musicological works.

Already published

Essay on the True Art of Playing Keyboard Instruments
C.P.E. BACH
ISBN 0 903873 14 1 Hardback
ISBN 0 903873 01 X Paperback

Ferruccio Busoni
EDWARD DENT
ISBN 0 90387 3 15 X Hardback
ISBN 0 90387 3 02 8 Paperback

Music, Men and Manners in France and Italy 1770
CHARLES BURNEY
ISBN 0 903873 16 8 Hardback
ISBN 0 903873 03 6 Paperback

My Musical Life
RIMSKY-KORSAKOV
ISBN 0 903873 13 3 Hardback
ISBN 0 903873 00 1 Paperback

A Mozart Pilgrimage
VINCENT & MARY NOVELLO
Edited by Nerina Medici and Rosemary Hughes
ISBN 0 903873 30 3 Hardback
ISBN 0 903873 10 9 Paperback

The Songs of Robert Schumann
ERIC SAMS
ISBN 0 903873 17 6 Hardback
ISBN 0 903873 18 4 Paperback

Varese : a Looking-Glass Diary
LOUISE VARESE
ISBN 0 903873 04 4 Paperback

Recently published

Pierre Boulez — Conversations with Celestin Deliege
ISBN 0 903873 21 4 Hardback
ISBN 0 903873 22 2 Paperback

The Recorder and its Music
EDGAR HUNT
ISBN 0 903873 31 1 Hardback
ISBN 0 903873 05 2 Paperback

Mozart's 'Don Giovanni'
HERMANN ABERT
ISBN 0 903873 19 2 Hardback
ISBN 0 903873 11 7 Paperback

Debussy — Impressionism and Symbolism
STEFAN JAROCINSKI
ISBN 0 903873 20 6 Hardback
ISBN 0 903873 09 5 Paperback

In preparation

Orchestral Variations
NORMAN DEL MAR

Pierre Boulez — A Symposium
Edited by WILLIAM GLOCK

Debussy Wagner
ROBIN HOLLOWAY

> A book by IAN KEMP on the life and music of
> Sir Michael Tippett is due to be published
> during 1978.

ERNST EULENBURG LTD   48 Great Marlborough Street · London W1V 2BN

PHILIPS

The Music of
SIR MICHAEL TIPPETT
conducted by
COLIN DAVIS

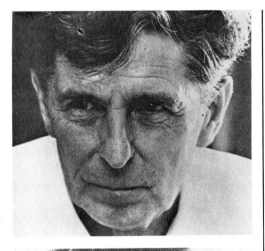

"One of the most individual & original composers of his generation."
Daily Telegraph

"Davis, unrivalled as a Tippett interpreter."
The Guardian

THE MIDSUMMER MARRIAGE
Carlyle/Harwood/Remedios
Burrows/Herincx
6703 027 (3-LP box set)
Recorded in association with the British Council and the Arts Council of Great Britain.

THE KNOT GARDEN
Barstow/Gomez/Minton
Tear/Herincx
6700 063 (2-LP box set)
Recorded in association with the Calouste Gulbenkian Foundation of Lisbon.

Both the above operas with the Chorus and Orchestra of The Royal Opera House, Covent Garden

PHILIPS

THE MIDSUMMER MARRIAGE: FOUR RITUAL DANCES
(From 6703 027)
CONCERTO FOR ORCHESTRA*
London Symphony Orchestra
6580 093
*Recorded in association with the British Council.

A CHILD OF OUR TIME
Norman/Baker/Cassilly
Shirley-Quirk
BBC Singers/BBC Choral Society
BBC Symphony Orchestra
6500 985

SYMPHONY NO.1
SUITE FOR THE BIRTHDAY OF PRINCE CHARLES
9500 107

SYMPHONY NO.3
Heather Harper
6500 662
The last three works recorded in association with the Rupert Foundation
and played by the London Symphony Orchestra

William Drummond

Covent Garden Gallery Ltd
20 Russell St *(By The Royal Opera House)*
London WC2   01-836 1139

Early British and European watercolours and oil paintings

Paul Sandby R.A. 1730-1809

Annually there will be a programme of exhibitions
in **Spring, Summer, Autumn** and at **Christmas**